Crucible is published quarterly by Hymns Ancient & Modern Ltd.
Registered Charity No. 270060

This publication is in collaboration with the Church of England's
Division of Mission and Public Affairs; the William Temple Foundation.

Editorial board

Stephen Platten, Edward Cardale, Kate Pearson, Elaine Graham,
Malcolm Brown, Chris Swift, Carol Wardman,
Matt Bullimore, James Woodward, Peter Scott, Simon Cuff, Jenny
Leith (Reviews Editor) and Jemima Lewis (Managing Editor).

Correspondence and articles

Correspondence and articles for submission should be sent to Jemima
Lewis at Hymns Ancient and Modern, periodicals@hymnsam.co.uk.
Articles should be of about 3,000 words.

Subscriptions

(for four copies): individual rate £22; institutions £40;
individual international £40; institutional international £50;
Single copies cost £7.
All prices included postage and packing. Cheques should
be made payable to Crucible, and sent to: Crucible subscriptions,
Subscription Manager, 13a Hellesdon Park Road, Norwich NR6 5DR.

Tel: 01603 785 910   Fax: 01603 624483.
crucible@hymnsam.co.uk

Direct Debit forms available from the same address

ISSN 0011-2100
ISBN 978-0-334-06327-8

Printed by The Five Castles Press, The Print Factory,
Raeburn Road South, Ipswich, Suffolk IP3 0ET

Contents

Editorial
Malcolm Brown   3

Articles

Responsible Investment and the Church   6
Commissioners for England
Bess Joffe

Where Your Treasure Is, There Your Heart   15
Will Be Also
Barbara Ridpath

Extractive Industries – A Case Study   26
on Investor Engagement
David Walker

Monotheism as a Foundation for Ethics   35
Jonathan Clatworthy

Forum

Churches and the Pandemic   48
Rob Marshall

Book Reviews   58

Editorial

Investing well to address an Environmental Crisis

World leaders gathered in Glasgow in November 2021 for the great climate conference, COP26, as the global build-up of greenhouse gasses reached a historic high.[1] The gap between talk and impact on the climate crisis seems as wide as ever. Meanwhile, the actions of protesters highlighting this gulf became more disruptive, with sitdowns on major motorways being followed by high-profile arrests and possible prison sentences. It feels as if climate change is becoming one of the battlegrounds in the much-vaunted culture wars of our time. Those with the power to effect change look for the kind of change that doesn't impact unduly on the electorate, whilst no action that can be taken in a real-world democracy appears to be sufficient to satisfy the single-issue campaigners.

But it would be wrong to assume that agency lies only with government on the one hand and activists on the other. Notwithstanding the numerous small actions that individuals and communities can take to reduce our impact on the environment, the sector of the economy that receives much attention, but which is hardest to hold to account, is the corporate world. Many would argue that it is the fundamental lack of accountability within current structures of the capitalist economy that prevent many of the measures which could have the greatest impact from ever happening.

This makes it all the more urgent to deploy any levers available to hold businesses – especially those involved in fossil fuels and other environmentally problematic sectors – to account. Shareholders have a vital role to play here, and the churches, as significant investors, need to weigh their moral duties alongside their fiduciary duty to make satisfactory returns which can support the work of the church on the ground.

It is a shame that the debate about the responsibilities of shareholders has polarised into a defence of maximising interest on the one hand (on the grounds that this supports the church to

Editorial

act locally) and total disinvestment, or divestment, on the other. Fundamentally, this is a familiar theological dilemma about Christian ethics in a fallen world. Should we prioritise purity, or effective transformation, when it is impossible to have both? In expressing this dilemma, the environmental activists are, perhaps, the new Puritans, although the church investors should probably not be characterised as Cavaliers, for reasons that this issue of Crucible should demonstrate! Sadly, we see too little actual debate. Instead the problem is too often presented as a simple binary: hold on to your shares or be denounced as a climate denier. It is to break out of this sterile impasse that this issue of Crucible has been put together.

Here, three of those at the centre of the Church of England's work on responsible and ethical investment set out their approach to maximising shareholder impact on corporate behaviours. The focus is on the Church of England because of its leading position as part of the Transition Pathway Initiative (of which more anon) and because its Ethical Investment Advisory Group (EIAG) is perhaps one of the most highly developed bodies approaching the field of ethical investment in a self-consciously theological way.

However, as the Chair of EIAG Barbara Ridpath notes, the EIAG includes representation from the Methodist Church which makes full use of the Group's policy recommendations, so the ecumenism of the Anglican-Methodist Covenant has some practical pay-back here. Moreover, it is hard to avoid the public perception that the Church Commissioners are "rolling in money", and that they are therefore the church shareholders with the greatest potential for leveraging their financial clout. And there is truth in this perception, although as Bess Joffe points out, the statutory commitment of the Commissioners is to invest their assets in order to generate revenue that supports the CofE's commitment to parish ministry in every community. Whilst the Commissioners are a very significant investor, even in the Church of England they are not the only player, and the EIAG develops ethical guidance for all the National Investing Bodies (NIBs).

In the somewhat strident debate about investor responsibility in the context of the climate crisis, and more widely in terms of ethical and responsible investing, the Church of England has addressed the theological tension between purity and pragmatic transformation with a clear bias toward transformation – whilst keeping the option of divestment (purity) up its sleeve to be deployed when corporate resistance to change proves incorrigible. Nor is this just a theoretical

Editorial

possibility. As David Walker outlines, when engaging with extractive industries, resistance to shareholder pressure proved, in one case, so impenetrable that divestment by the Church of England followed – precipitating more widespread divestment from that company and, ultimately, a moderation of their environmentally and socially harmful practices.

The ability of a major shareholder like the Church of England to change the way corporations behave through judicious deployment of the power of their shareholding tends to be under-appreciated. Much engagement happens, of necessity, privately and away from the public or media gaze. This edition of Crucible helps to make the case for a pragmatic yet theological approach to transforming corporate behaviours, as a contribution to public debate about the tactics of combatting climate change.

However, the ethics of investment policy extend to many other morally problematic arenas, and the EIAG's current work focusses on Big Tech and the power of the tech giants, through to the application of Artificial Intelligence, Machine Learning and so on, to do both public good, and also serious public harm. Whether the Big Tech industry is capable of transformation for good is a question that investors continue to grapple with. It surely needs more exploration in the future.

Malcolm Brown is the Director of Mission and Public Affairs for the Archbishops' Council of the Church of England and a member of the Ethical Investment Advisory Group. He has guest-edited this edition of Crucible.

Notes

1. https://www.bbc.co.uk/news/science-environment-59016075 accessed 25 October 2021.

Responsible Investment and the Church Commissioners for England

BESS JOFFE

Saving the planet from the effects of climate change is not just a job for activists, but for us all. Politicians, citizens, we all have a part to play. As investors, particularly as investors with Christian values, it's vital that we consider the world we will be faced with tomorrow and consider what we can do to make sure it's a world we will be proud to leave behind. That's why we take issues relating to people and the planet with the utmost seriousness.

Balancing this responsibility alongside our obligations and long-term outlook is key to our strategy. The Church Commissioners for England, which manage a £9.2bn investment fund, exist to support the mission and ministry of the Church of England in perpetuity.

We aim to create long-term financial returns through the investment portfolio. Those returns help fund some activities of churches, cathedrals, local parishes and dioceses, which deliver the Church's mission in its most direct way.

The investment fund's proceeds contribute more than £300m to the Church every year, more than 15% of the Church's annual running costs, which makes the Commissioners among the largest charitable givers in the UK.

Each year, that money is used to:
- Fund mission activities
- Support ministry costs in dioceses with fewer resources
- Fund bishops' and some cathedral costs
- Administer the legal framework for reorganising parishes and settling the future of closed church buildings

- Pay clergy pensions for service prior to 1998
- Provide some of the vital financial resources required for our 12,500 parishes.

In addition to providing funding for the Church, we make sure that the way we invest, and what we invest in, bring benefits to the wider world. In this way our assets can work hardest to change things for the better. We invest in line with Christian values, centred on the Church of England's five marks of mission, and our approach is to invest in ways that respect people and respect the planet.

Since the fund will support the Church in perpetuity, we look to invest the money entrusted to us for future generations, as well as for today's parishes and parishioners. This long term approach has seen a positive income, or returns, for the past decade. That has in turn enabled the Commissioners to significantly increase distributions to the Church in recent years. Longer-term results were also strong, with performance over five, ten and 30 years all ahead of our target returns. This long-term approach has also meant that despite the Covid-19 pandemic, the Church Commissioners will continue to distribute £900m over the next three year cycle (2023-25).

As a faith-based investor we are not only value driven in terms of the returns we need to support the Church, but we are also able to choose our investments in line with strict ethical frameworks. This enables the Commissioners to get the best of both worlds and continue to engage with companies in line with our ethical principles.

There has never been a greater need for responsible and ethical investment. It has become increasingly clear that companies and investors must act now to combat climate change and the social challenges highlighted by Covid-19.

This year the Church Commissioners became a signatory to the UK Stewardship code, having met the requirements as laid out by the UK Financial Reporting Council, a body that sets the UK's corporate governance and stewardship guidelines to promote transparency and integrity in business. Only 23 asset owners became signatories this year by meeting the high standards for investing money.

We have cared about environmental, social and governance (ESG) issues for many years and certainly long before it was fashionable to do so! We continue to be ambitious, leading by example and we are proud to be at the forefront of responsible investment and able to partner with other key players to make change across the real economy.

Being credible and authentic in our aspirations to make change is very important to us, and we are humbled when our efforts are recognised. This month, we were recognised for Excellence in ESG by the British Private Equity & Venture Capital Association for our work and engagement on climate change, diversity and inclusion. As investors in funds that manage private companies, through investing capital into companies that are not publicly listed, the Commissioners have a powerful role in steering what environmental and social considerations their investment managers focus on when investing in or buying private companies.

The UN-backed Principles for Responsible Investment (a member organization with nearly 4,000 signatories around the globe) graded the Commissioners A+ for Responsible Investment Strategy & Governance, following an annual assessment in 2020 and gained A+ ratings for Manager Selection, Appointment and Monitoring for all asset classes. We were rated A for engagement and voting, and for our management of our directly held property assets. A key highlight for us, and acknowledgment of the hard work of the teams, was being included in the PRI's Leaders' Group for the second year in a row.

It is our goal to help shape, lead and innovate. We know that in order to be a leader, we must ensure that we have a thoughtful and impactful strategy.

In 2020, we reviewed our responsible investment priorities and grounded our future work in two areas of focus: Respect for the Planet and Respect for People. These pillars give a focus and foundation for our responsible investment decision making. This broader scope of work will allow us to meet the challenges of the next decade as responsible, ethical and long-term investors who are focused on helping the fund achieve sustainable returns.

Respect for the Planet

We regard climate change as a vital issue for responsible investors and we strive to safeguard the integrity of creation in line with the Church's Fifth Mark of Mission. "Respect for the Planet" is the grounding for our climate change efforts and issues related to natural capital, where natural capital can be defined as the world's stocks of natural assets which include geology, soil, air, water and all living things.

The climate crisis is so profound, and so urgent, that it dominates our responsible investment agenda. As part of our Christian calling, we are firmly committed to achieving net zero carbon within our portfolio of investments and leading a "just transition" so no people or communities are left behind as the planet moves to a low carbon economy. We achieve these aims through robust engagement, investing in solutions to help bring about that low carbon economy, and challenging ourselves to do more and better every day.

Our approach is multi-faceted. It starts with engagement to effect real world change by using the power of our voice to encourage companies to make the changes the world needs to achieve a just transition to net zero. If companies don't make the changes we require, we restrict them from being investible and divest from any we might still hold. The National Investing Bodies, including the Church Commissioners, made a commitment at General Synod in 2018 to divest from fossil fuel companies that are not making changes to transition in line with the goals of the Paris Agreement by 2023, and we will absolutely follow through with this pledge.

For example, 12 companies made changes to their strategy and operations in 2020 in response to the NIBs' extensive engagement regarding alignment to the Paris Agreement, while nine that didn't were divested. Any remaining fossil fuel companies in our investment portfolio that not aligned with the Paris Agreement goals by 2023 will be divested.

Divestment on its own comes with significant risks. Voices who challenge companies to change are making a real difference, and by divesting we would remove our ability as shareholders to have a voice. We cannot be silent on the matter of climate change. The risks are too high.

As the Archbishop of Canterbury, Justin Welby, told the Today Programme earlier this month, he is "very comfortable that we are engaging with the fossil fuel industry companies, provided they change and have a net zero target in a reachable horizon in the near future."

We work with the global investment community, through collaboration with our investment peers including the other Church of England National Investing Bodies ('NIBs'), to engage with large parts of the global economy and bring them in line with a transition to a low carbon world. This has enabled us to have meaningful and impactful roles in leading the investment community to align with the risks and opportunities presented by the climate crisis.

We are active participants in Climate Action 100+, the largest-ever investor climate coalition in history (focused on engaging with the largest carbon emitters to influence change), with 615 investors and US$ 55 trillion of assets under management (2/3 of the global economy). Climate Action 100+ is underpinned by assessments from the Transition Pathway Initiative (TPI). The Church Commissioners and the Church of England Pensions Board had a leading role in founding TPI, which is now supported by over 110 funds and investors with a combined $40 trillion of assets under management or advisement.

By using our voice with our investee companies, policymakers, and our peers in the investment industry, we can make and have made a real and demonstrable impact on the global economy. A recent example of successful engagement is where we actively worked with other investors to replace non-executive directors on ExxonMobil's board. In June, three new directors were voted onto the board, the culmination of a successful six-month campaign of active engagement. If the newly constituted board does not make the changes we require, we would expect to divest.

Over the next three years, our environmental efforts are expanding and will increasingly focus on biodiversity, which we have identified as the next most pressing issue for us as investors and as landowners. While the risks associated with biodiversity loss are significant, on the positive side global biodiversity policy is expected to tighten, with a UN-led Global Biodiversity Framework expected to be signed in October. As such, this issue is ripe for investor focus and engagement and we are confident that strides can be made.

As a universal owner, with a diverse range of investments across sectors, biodiversity loss and ecosystem collapse pose significant threats, not only to the planet but also to the economy and the Commissioners' investment portfolio in the same way climate change does.

Investor efforts to tackle biodiversity loss are still at an early stage and we will consider whether to focus on specific sectors or particular geographical regions of the world as we delve into the issue. Given our portfolio make-up and the links to our work on climate change, we feel we have an opportunity to positively influence the discourse on biodiversity loss, support best practices in this nascent area, and have a direct positive impact through our land holdings.

Responsible Investment and the Church Commissioners for England

Respect for People

Our second pillar and area of focus addresses the fourth mark of mission, what we call "Respect for People". This theme encompasses our existing approach to human rights and modern slavery, and there is more that we will do in this area. Since 2017, societies around the world have seen the rise of the #MeToo movement, followed by Black Lives Matter and the Covid-19 pandemic. These societal catalysts are creating challenges for employees, employers and communities in ways that will affect them and their investors over the next decade.

The Commissioners' global leadership on the environmental impacts of climate change will now be expanded to address the impacts of the shift to a low-carbon economy on people to ensure a just transition for communities that are impacted. We have been engaging companies on the issue of climate justice, ensuring that the world's most vulnerable are not left behind and are appropriately supported in the low-carbon transition.

We have also worked collaboratively to address key systemic issues which benefit from collective engagement, such as the interface between Big Tech and human rights. Our approach is being shaped by the review currently undertaken by the EIAG (the Ethical Investment Advisory Group).

We work closely with The Clewer Initiative on campaigns to raise awareness of modern slavery. We arrange seminars with rural stakeholders, which have resulted in the development of a phone app, in eight languages, to get the message out to farmers and workers about the risk of modern slavery. The Farm Work Welfare App, launched in July 2020, and endorsed by the National Farmers' Union, includes information on what to look out for, and allows users to report concerns to the UK's 24-hour modern slavery helpline.

Recognising current societal issues is a key part of any responsible investment approach. Covid-19 has given rise to a series of challenges to workforces around the world and moved the use of technology forward at a much faster pace than was foreseeable only a year ago. This trend will continue especially when we look ahead to the future of technology and consider the risks that entails. One example is the risk that artificial intelligence and robots could replace workers, a risk very likely to grow.

In order to mitigate against significant labour disruption, we plan to engage with companies in the sectors most likely to face these challenges, to understand what they are doing to protect jobs and retrain employees. Building on this knowledge, we hope to be able to create a best practices framework and establish a set of investor expectations of companies that others can also leverage.

The final component to our Respect for People pillar is a renewed focus on diversity and inclusion. While strides have been made for gender diversity across some jurisdictions, much remains to be done on both gender and ethnic diversity across the board. We plan to challenge companies to move beyond mere representation, and to embrace diversity and inclusion as a value-add both for their culture and for their bottom lines. Our proxy voting supports this focus and engagement will follow.

Supporting these two pillars

While we have defined these two pillars, we support them with other efforts across our responsible investment work. One way we do this is with our governance analysis. Assessing board composition, capital protection and shareholder rights is an important element of our work and informs how we seek to influence change at companies. We also assess engagement opportunities with individual companies whose performance may lag their peers and who are not appropriately managing ESG risks. In rare cases, these engagements may escalate into a more public, 'activist stewardship' approach, like our engagement with Exxon.

A key governance mechanism we use to encourage change within companies is through the annual shareholder voting process. Voting is one of the fundamental shareholder rights which we leverage to shape companies' policies, encourage good governance and hold boards and senior management teams to account. Our ability to vote is also a key incentive for us to stay invested in companies that we might otherwise wish to divest. A seat at the table with company executives and boards is powerful and enables engagement. We believe it is far better for investors who wish to make a difference keep challenging companies than sell out of a company for the stock to be purchased by those who do not share our values.

We have a voting policy that sets out our approach to voting on issues including executive pay, governance, diversity, modern slavery, audit, climate change policy, tax and employee pay. We expect boards to uphold best practice for addressing ESG issues as well as demonstrate risk oversight aligned with shareholder returns.

Responsible Investment and the Church Commissioners for England

While we will use our vote on a wide range of issues, the main areas that trigger dissenting votes are executive pay, auditor independence and board composition. On executive pay, most of our dissent votes this year were triggered by executive pay schemes that failed to integrate environmental, social and governance issues into their variable pay schemes, or when we considered companies' short-term awards to be excessive. This is particularly prevalent in US markets, where executive pay is outsized compared with other markets.

Finally, our approach is grounded in advice from the Church of England's Ethical Investment Advisory Group (EIAG). The EIAG provides timely and practical advice on a range of issues that are relevant to investing in a way that is distinctly Christian and Anglican. The Commissioners work closely with the EIAG, seeking their advice on challenging issues and using this advice to inform our investment policies. We can then apply these policies, for example, for exclusions.

For example, we exclude from direct investments companies involved in indiscriminate weaponry, conventional weaponry, non-military firearms, pornography, tobacco, alcohol, gambling, high interest rate lending, extraction of thermal coal and production of oil from oil sands, subject to revenue thresholds.

We also advocate for change beyond dialogue with individual companies. We do this by working through industry associations to engage with policymakers, regulators, and legislators. We work closely with Bishops in the House of Lords and the Second Church Estates Commissioner in Parliament, to assess bills related to ESG matters, and respond to regulatory consultations.

Investing in solutions

We seek to clarify our understanding of the environmental and social impact that our investment portfolio has on the world. This is why we believe in impact investing. Impact investing is buying shares in companies, public or private, that are intended to generate positive, measurable social and environmental impact alongside a financial return. We won IPE Magazine's inaugural award for Best in Impact Investing in 2020.

We have invested £1.1bn in impactful solutions, which represents around 11.5% of the portfolio, with £630mm of this invested in climate solutions (as at year end 2020). This compares favourably to peers.

The Church Commissioners has demanding but exciting financial objectives for 2021, and we also are serious about our goal to create real change. Through our pillars of Respect for People and Respect for the Planet, we plan to expand our activities to fulfil our ethical and Christian duties. As we carry out this work, we are aware that it is a great privilege as well as a responsibility. We pray that God will give us wisdom and humility as we serve Him and the Church in the year ahead. For people, for the planet, for the long term.

Bess Joffe is Head of Responsible Investment for the Church Commissioners for England.

Where Your Treasure Is, There Your Heart Will Be Also [1]

Barbara Ridpath

Introduction

How we use our money is both an outworking of our beliefs and an act of witness. This is true for individuals, communities and church institutions. In every instance, we have both the right and the responsibility to speak into the public debate and to help develop a shared understanding of the values that are important to us as a society. As Christians, our values are grounded in our beliefs and our theology, though depending on one's religious tradition and personal beliefs this can be quite a 'broad church,' with many different interpretations of what these beliefs include and the way they are lived.

Working with others who share similar beliefs and principles helps our money create an enormous force for change. We have seen this over time in many areas. Leadership from the church has played an integral part in the growth of the ESG (environmental, social and governance) movement in the United Kingdom and beyond. Yet the moral leadership that comes from the church is not without its own perils. We risk being caught in contradictions between what we say and what we do, and some of the most fraught disagreements are among people, all trying to do good, with different approaches to the best way to achieve change.

The way in which the Church of England's money is invested is an integral part of its witness and mission. Christian theology and stewardship inform how these investment duties are performed by those responsible.

This article addresses the background, history and evolution of the Church of England's engagement as an investor, focusing on the theological underpinnings that drive its reasoning. It considers the effectiveness of engagement and divestment. The article concludes by looking at some of the issues and challenges the future may hold.

Background, history and evolution of the Church of England's investment engagement

The Church of England, largely for historical reasons, holds funds from a variety of sources for manifold purposes. These can range from cash from collections at the local level, gifts and endowments, and money to pay the pensions of staff and clergy. Some are used quickly for current spending. Others are invested as a permanent endowment in order to provide a return that gives the Church a source of income. As a function of the purpose of the funds, their statutes and regulation, the investment time horizons of the funds can differ, as can their investment strategies. As a result, the combination of investments among cash, shares in listed companies, funds or private equity and bonds will differ depending upon the Church bodies investing and the end use of the funds. If we consider the parable of the talents (Mathew 25:14-30), each of these bodies is expected to produce a return on its money to fulfil its purposes and enable the Church to function.

Three main central bodies invest on behalf of the Church of England. They are: the Church Commissioners for England who hold a permanent endowment, the vast majority of the income from which goes to support the ministry of the parishes.[2] the Pensions Board which provides pensions and retirement housing for clergy and staff from the results of the investment of their funds and the CBF Church of England Funds which holds a substantial proportion of the investments of parishes, dioceses and cathedrals, managed by CCLA, an investment manager. Collectively, these three are known as the National Investing Bodies of the Church or NIBs.

The Church Commissioners' first established a form of ethical investment policy in 1948 when they began to invest in public equities and avoided shares in companies involved in gambling, tobacco and arms. Today they are advised by the Ethical Investment Advisory Group (EIAG), which was established in 1994 following a court challenge from the Bishop of Oxford who wanted the Commissioners' to restrict investment in all companies with subsidiaries in South Africa. The court ruled in favour of the Commissioners' but held that ethical investment could be accommodated if a particular investment would be in conflict with the objects of the charity.[3] The EIAG was formed in order to advise the NIBs on appropriate investments aligned with their Christian values and objects. Its terms of reference and activities have changed over the last nearly 30 years, as the NIBs have expanded their teams while they and institutional investors more generally have developed expertise in ethical and responsible investment. As stated in the 2018 revision of the EIAG's terms of reference, 'The EIAG's purpose is to support the NIBs to invest ethically in a way which is distinctly Christian. This shall be achieved by offering timely and practical Advice and support to the NIBs, who shall formulate policy.'[4]

Membership of the EIAG is by appointment of the Nominations Committee of the EIAG, which seeks candidates with multidisciplinary backgrounds in business, investment, theology or other areas that contribute to the quality of the debate and discussion within the group. It seeks both diversity and wide-ranging views, so that it can represent the Church in its broadest sense. For this reason, in addition to members and observers appointed by the NIBs, there are other observers who attend and contribute. Of particular note is the intentional inclusion of an observer from Joint Advisory Committee on the Ethics of Investment, which provides advice on ethical issues to the Central Finance Board of the Methodist Church. This formal, ecumenical link is central to the EIAG's commitment to arriving at advice than can be accepted and used within the wider church community.

A Secretariat provides the essential research, writing, and administrative tasks to support the Group. Originally, the EIAG produced advice largely around investment prohibitions, a series of 'thou shalt nots' on certain key sectors that the Church felt it could not support, such as alcohol, tobacco and firearms. Unsurprisingly, as the EIAG and the NIBs began to look at investment issues through the lens of Christian theology, myriad other issues arose. Today the EIAG's advice ranges from issues of executive remuneration, supply chains, Genetically Modified Organisms (GMOs), to most importantly climate change. It also offers advice on areas such as different asset classes where straightforward ethical restrictions are more difficult to apply, and will soon include a major piece of advice on the technology, or Big Tech industry. All these positions are publicly available on the Church of England's website.[5]

The policies are publicly available in order that others may benefit from what we have learned in our work, whether these be other investors, other Church members, or any other body with concerns about how their money is used. In each case, the advice includes the theological grounding on which the advice is based. Making the advice pubic is a key way that the Church is able to 'punch above its weight' in the area of ethical investing, as the EIAG advice, together with the NIBs policy, informs the positions of a wide range of other investors around the world. In turn, the EIAG also looks widely at research and work that is going on outside the EIAG to inform its own views and opinions.

The EIAG's work programme is determined by requests for advice that come from the NIBs, issues that arise from EIAG members directly, as well as a regular 'horizon scanning' exercise that keeps us informed and aware of issues that we should consider. The EIAG is also mindful of views expressed in Synod and in other Church forums that warrant consideration.

Theological Foundations

In order to invest in line with their charitable objects and meet their fidicuiary and other legal duties to their beneficiaries, the NIBs need advice on the practical application of Christian teaching, tradition and reason in the investment world. This is not easy; the answers to many subjects do not fall neatly out of a direct reading of the Bible. Many of the issues it confronts, from the peaceful use of nuclear power, to genetic engineering were not foreseen there. However, most of the principles on which we can base our judgements can be found there, since human behaviour and human flaws have been around since the creation of humankind, or at least since the Fall.

For this reason, the EIAG tends to turn to the first principles of Christian theology. As Christians, we believe human beings are made in the image of God and, in Jesus Christ, are called to know God and to participate in the divine life. All of the EIAG's Advice seeks to draw out what "made in the image of God" means through four theological principles. We believe we are all called to:

1 Flourish as persons: that is, we are given freedom in order that we can flourish (even if we also use our freedom to do evil). We are given irredeemable dignity which must be protected and should not be threatened or undermined.

2 Flourish in relationship: people are naturally social beings—whatever enhances their relationships will enable them to flourish, whatever harms their relationships or causes hatred or division will inevitability diminish them. This means that we are also called to help

communities grow and flourish.

3 Stand with the marginalised: throughout the Bible, there is a consistent refrain that God has a special concern for those who are vulnerable or excluded from society, and all of us have a duty to stand with those who suffer from all abuses of power.

4 Serve the common good: society and the individual organisations that make it up are to serve community and not their own private good—when this fails, it is the responsibility of other bodies, including the Government, to ensure they do.

These principles are also summed up well by the former Governor of the Bank of England, Mark Carney in his recent book Value(s), where he writes 'a sense of self must be accompanied by a sense of solidarity.'[6] The first principle is about a sense of self in the image of God, while the others consider how we treat all people of all faiths, both because all were created in the image of God, and because we are here to build the Kingdom of God on earth.

Beyond these four principles that relate to being made in the image of God and consider both how we behave and how we treat others, the Bible calls us very clearly to be stewards of God's creation (Genesis 1:26-28). This gives us a responsibility to care for the earth and for all who dwell upon it and within its waters as well as its plant life. This is the fifth principle around which the EIAG grounds its theological reasoning.[7]

It is easy enough to find verses in the Bible telling us to sell all we have and give it to the poor in order to be a follower of Jesus (Matthew 19:21), and easy also to play 'duelling Bible verses' when discussing theology. So these principles keep the EIAG grounded while thinking over any issue that arises on the Church's investments. They enable us to focus on matters that are genuinely relevant to us, where we can add the most value, and ensure that we try to be consistent in our approach over time.

However straightforward the application of these principles might be to issues such as advice on addictive substances or the environment, they are often less obvious when trying to address advice on extractive industries or supply chains. Even in the most straightforward cases, preparing the advice requires a core understanding of the subject, and of the ramifications (including any unintended consequences) of the advice for a reasoned application of the theology.

As this body of theological reasoning has developed, the EIAG's advice has been useful not only to the NIBs, but to the wider body of Church investors and other investors in no small part due to its grounding in Christian theology. The voice of Church investors tends to have an outsized influence on markets relative to the size of funds actually managed by the Church bodies. One reason for this is the ability of the NIBs to build coalitions of like-minded investors engaging with the management and boards of companies in which they are invested. The following section discusses how this happens.

Methods of Engagement

Investing bodies can seek to influence outcomes in a variety of ways. Among the possible techniques, some of the most frequently used include:
- direct engagement with the boards and executives in the companies they own including proxy voting and filing shareholder resolutions,
- in the mandates they give to and discussions they have with those who manage their money,
- collaboration with other like-minded investors,
- speaking out publicly on key issues, and engaging with policy makers, and
- divestment of shares or prohibitions on investments.

Direct engagement may involve a variety of actions. It can start with sharing the investing bodies' concerns in a reasoned way with the management of companies in which they hold shares, often prioritised by a combination of: 1) the importance of their concern, 2) the importance of their holding, and 3) the expectation of influence. This may start with letters, and move on to meeting and ultimately to the possibility of initiating or participating in shareholder resolutions. The objective is to get the company's management to understand the investor's perspective and bring about management action that changes the company's behaviours.

This is often most effectively done when investors and company management can exchange and explore ideas privately, permitting the company to enact or announce change as their own initiative, and providing a demonstration effect for other companies who face the same issue. Ideally resolutions filed by investors are then supported by company management rather than opposed.

Where private, individual engagement does not work, it is often useful to collaborate with other, like-minded investors to demonstrate the degree to which asset owners all agree that a change is needed. This can occur either publicly or privately. Increasing the percentage representation of ownership engaged in trying to change a company's policy, especially if these investors demonstrate their willingness to use their power and influence in the way they vote in annual meetings can have a marked effect on their persuasiveness.

Public engagement may be used when investors are unsuccessful privately or when investors wish to demonstrate the breadth and depth of public support for a position.

All of these techniques have been used for varying purposes. The EIAG began its work making investment prohibitions on certain key sectors that the Church felt it could not commit capital to or derive profit from such as alcohol, tobacco and firearms. However, where there is not a direct prohibition on investment, the NIBs have found engagement to be a much more effective way of inciting change than divestment, which is used only as a last choice option, when all other methods fail.

Divestment means the withholding of capital (debt or equity) from a particular company for non-financial reasons. These reasons may include misalignment with the investors values or objects, concern that continued investment will alienate beneficiaries and/or supporters or a desire to influence social norms. Divestment (if made public) can be effective in highlighting awareness however it rarely yields change to company behaviour. Once an asset owner divests, the investor loses all leverage with the company, and all means of speaking to the company. The new holder of the asset may not share the same ethical concerns and the divested company will be able to continue its behaviour unchecked. The impact of public equity divestment is greater when companies actually are likely to need to raise new equity from the stock markets. However, given the miniscule amount of new money that is raised through the equity markets these days – especially for the oil and gas sector who predominately look to the debt markets for capital, divestment of equity does little to impede the actions of the company in question and on its own, does not brings systemic change to systemic issues such as climate change.

This is not to say that divestment has not been effective in certain circumstances, notably when it catalyses consumer boycotts and escalates political pressure, such as in the campaigns against tobacco or against apartheid in South Africa in the 1970-90s. In both these cases the stigma created by these campaigns catalysed significant political, social and regulatory pressure. However, divestment also carries risks of unintended consequences. In particular, in the current debate over divestment in all oil companies, two of the possible outcomes include: the sale of these assets to privately held companies or hedge funds that care only about profit maximization and little about decarbonizing our world, and a depressed share price that makes the company susceptible to takeover by investors who do not care about the environmental consequences of their investment. Odey Asset Management's founder Crispin Odey recently noted that it was easy to make money from fossil fuel companies, saying 'they [big institutional investors] are so keen to get rid of oil assets, they're leaving fantastic returns on the table.' [8]

To date, the NIBs have developed expertise in public engagement, notably around issues of climate change, but also around the extractive industries, and combined with the stick of divestment, engagement has proved an extremely effective strategy. Most recently the Church Commissioners were engaged in meaningfully re-shaping the board of directors of Exxon in order to try and change that companies policies on adapting to climate change. It was an unprecedented achievement for investors and the Commissioners' have been clear and publicly stated they will divest if those policies do not change. In a very different manner, all the NIBs helped create the Transition Pathway Initiative, a global, asset-owner led initiative which assesses companies' preparedness for the transition to a low carbon economy. In addition, the Pensions Board was instrumental in the launch in early 2020 of FTSE TPI Climate Transition Index, which enables investors seeking greater alignment to the goals of the Paris Agreement to gain exposure to the opportunities that companies can generate from the transition to a low carbon economy.

Of course, the church more broadly has myriad ways of engaging. There are grassroots campaigns on social issues such as refugee policy and providing homes for refugees. The Green Church movement is helping churches around the world make their churches more environmentally friendly and helping to raise awareness of key climate change issues. In addition, the moral authority of church leaders can be powerful, whether it is one of the Archbishops, the Bishops in the House of Lords speaking for children, or on the impact of technology. In an ideal world, all interested parties within the Church would be able to clearly and calmly discuss and debate issues around key ethical topics in order to arrive at a common position. This would be invaluable as these views would have much more impact if the Church spoke with one voice. However, the nature of people's assets and interests means that everyone's views will not always be aligned. An individual investor, recognising he or she alone will have little voice at a shareholders' meeting may opt for unitized investments where the manager's views align with the investor, or may feel divestment makes most sense.

Collaboration with Others

Religious leaders can use their moral authority in collaboration with others. Just recently, in advance of COP26, the Archbishop of Canterbury, together with the Pope and the Ecumenical Patriarch Bartholomew issued a joint statement on the urgency of climate change action.[9]

Church groups were some of the first to engage in responsible investing, with groups like the Church Investors Group (CIG), the Ecumenical Centre for Corporate Responsibility (ECCR) and the Interfaith Center on Corporate Responsibility (ICCR), all active in providing moral leadership across denominations and boundaries on investment issues. Over time, to increase their influence, some organisations have broadened their membership beyond church investors and people of faith to any and all who support their principles. Sometimes this has required a shift in their principles away from those based in Christian theology to a broader, more generic values-based approach.

Whether building broad-based coalitions, or narrower specifically religious-based groupings, these organisations are helping get messages to business and government on what matters to them, and how they would like their money used. This is most effective when these groups have a deep understanding of the issue at hand, can discuss issues in clear, fact-based ways, and understand the objectives of the businesses they are speaking to. Acting in coalition with broad-based consumer support can bring added strength.

Conclusion

The Church of England has been a catalyst for change. It has brought with it a huge swathe of investors who are also seeking to use their money to affect change as a function of both best practice, and of the values of those investors, who may be of many faiths or no faith. The EIAG faces multiple challenges, the foremost of which is its future role in the wider field of ethical investing. It is working hard to move from a 'though shalt not' approach to an active partner that supports and encourages positive developments in the markets, whether these are alternative energy sources, impact investing, new corporate forms or improved governance that restores public confidence in business.

The EIAG is thinking about how to address new challenges, such as the extensive use of bond finance and private equity: these receive significantly less scrutiny than public equity investments in spite of the fact that they have been much more significant providers of capital to business over the last several years. At the same time, the EIAG needs to keep a long-term vision in a world where the speed of change is accelerating. It needs to find and keep its distinctively Christian voice in the burgeoning world of ethical and impact investing. It needs to do all of this while trying not to impede the NIBs from optimising their investment returns so as to ensure the Church has the financial resources it needs to serve its mission. Most of all, it needs to find a way to create dialogue with church members on their views, and spend more time in outreach to members.

Fortunately, the EIAG is gifted with a diverse panel of enormous talent, as well as wise advisers and the staff and boards of the National Investing Bodies who live and work in the markets daily. All these people believe and understand the value of targeted advice, grounded in Christian theology, as an aid in their policy formulation.

Barbara Ridpath is the Chair of the Ethical Investment Advisory Group. She spent her career in finance in New York, London and Paris, but in recent years has turned her attention to the intersection of theology and finance. She is enormously grateful for the research and editorial support of Anna McDonald, Secretary to the EIAG, and for some writing done by Professor Robert Song for the EIAG, in the preparation of this paper.

Notes

1. Matthew 6:21.
2. The Church Commissioners were established from Queen Anne's Bounty, a scheme set up in 1704 to enable the purchase of land

to augment the livings of poor clergy and the Ecclesiastical Commissioners.

3. Harries v The Church Commissioners for England [1992] 1 WLR 1241.

4. Ethical Investment Advisory Group's Terms of Reference. (https://www.churchofengland.org/about/leadership-and-governance/ethical-investment-advisory-group) last accessed 13 September 2021.

5. https://www.churchofengland.org/about/leadership-and-governance/ethical-investment-advisory-group/policies-and-reviews last accessed 9 October 2021.

6. Carney, Mark. Value(s): *Building a Better World for All*. London: William Collins, 2021. P.6.

7. EIAG Annual Review 2020/21, p. 9. (https://www.churchofengland.org/sites/default/files/2021-07/Annual%20Review%202020_21.pdf) last accessed 4 October 2021.

8. https://www.ft.com/content/ed11c971-be02-47dc-875b-90762b35080e last accessed 9 October 2021.

9. https://www.archbishopofcanterbury.org/sites/abc/files/2021-09/Joint%20Statement%20on%20the%20Environment.pdf last accessed 4 October 2021.

Extractive Industries — A Case Study on Investor Engagement

David Walker

Introduction

Extractive industries lie at the core of the global economy. From copper for cabling to rare Earth metals for specialist components in mobile phones, and from industrial aggregates for construction to gem stones for the jewellery trade, natural resources in huge quantities are taken from the Earth each year for human use. In many parts of the Global South, natural resources, of which extractable materials are a major constituent, present one of the best opportunities to generate revenue in hard currencies, money which can then be applied to support wider economic development and to sustain social programmes such as health and education.

In earlier years, when the focus was on avoiding "sin stocks" such as tobacco or weaponry, the sector had not been a priority for the EIAG or the National Investment Bodies of the Church, as neither the concept of extraction nor the products derived from it raised direct ethical issues. However, as the EIAG became increasingly focused on improving ethical practice through informed engagement with companies, the risks associated with business practices, together with the opportunities for positive influence in the Extractives sector, moved into the spotlight.

By its very nature, extractive industry is strongly linked to place. Natural resources can only be taken from where they lie, and many of the most valuable resources are to be found in the Global South. Extraction has huge impacts on the places where it is based. As was the case in the expansion of coal mining in the UK in the late 19th and early 20th centuries, entire towns can be created to service the lifespan of a mine. Longitudinally, the physical after-effects of mining – from high unemployment to displaced populations to large tailings

Extractive Industries – A Case Study on Investor Engagement

dams – may remain long after the mine has closed. Meanwhile, the profits generated during extraction are shared between the companies concerned and (usually) the national state within which the extraction site lies. They may have been spent, reinvested elsewhere, released as shareholder dividends, or corruptly laundered, long before the full costs to the local community and environment are realised.

It would not have been possible to undertake advice and policy work on extraction without engaging in depth with the many interested parties concerned. We were hugely grateful to those who turned up in person in London to participate in round table events and to others who participated by video conferencing links. We were especially appreciative of the church leaders, company staff, trade unions and community representatives, who all gave generously of their time to meet with the small delegation of us who undertook the study tour of South Africa and Zambia which lay at the heart of our gathering of information and deepening of understanding.

The key ethical risks of extraction

Five broad areas of ethical risk emerged from this extensive process of stakeholder engagement: human rights; health and safety; corruption and taxation; environment and ecology; social and economic concerns. Underpinning these was an awareness of the importance of good governance practices to reduce risk, and of companies taking responsibility for the impact of their operations throughout the life cycle of extraction and, where restoration work is required, beyond it.

1. Human rights concerns can arise when indigenous communities are forcibly displaced from their homes and lands in order to accommodate mining activities. Such communities, especially when far away from the seat of government, often have little or no political influence at the national and international levels where substantive decisions are taken. Communities can be harassed by mining staff where their presence or activities are felt to be detrimental, or add costs, to the extraction process. Even in the West, nations are reluctant to allow the immediate surrounding community to operate a veto over mining operations. One need look no further for an example than the UK government's insistence on seeing the licensing of fracking operations as a national matter, excluded from local government control. However, as the Vedanta case discussed later illustrates, these concerns affect

communities at an even deeper level when what is being proposed constitutes the permanent destruction of ancestral lands that may have been settled and farmed by a particular community for as far back as its history is recorded, and which may contain sacred sites and places hallowed by the bones of earlier generations.

2. Health and safety issues include both workplace and community impacts. Healthy and safety legislation can vary hugely from country to country, and even where laws exist they may not always be complied with or enforced. Extractive industries are especially prone to hazards related to operating very large machinery, underground working, or operations on unstable sites such as tailings from previously mined materials. Communities can be at risk of tailings dams collapsing onto inhabited areas long after active working has ceased. Whilst large corporations will have health and safety standards and policies in place, these may not always be followed in practice by the joint venture companies in which they are stakeholders working at local level. Moreover, mining sites often attract informal artisanal activity either on site or nearby. Such operations are entirely unregulated, and often highly unsafe. On our Zambian visit we saw young boys climbing almost vertical, and dangerously unstable, tailings slopes in search of minerals to be laundered via local markets into the legal supply chain.

3. Corruption and taxation is an area of particular concern. Corruption can be at national level, with joint venture companies structured so as to direct profits to politically favoured individuals and families, or at a more local level. Our site visits identified evidence of official community representatives being given generous and exclusive contracts to provide services to the mine in return for suppressing local opposition. Governments typically operate a system of royalty payments based on the amount of material extracted, which are then considered part of general taxation without any effort to apply funds directly to defray the negative impacts of operations on the local environment and community. Studies have also shown that the amount of materials entering the world market can be significantly higher than the amounts declared for tax purposes, suggesting that customs declarations are not always full and complete. The EIAG has separate advice on taxation issues where these are not specific to the extractive sector.

Extractive Industries – A Case Study on Investor Engagement

4. Environmental and ecological risks include both the choice of site and the impact of mining on it. Commercial pressure can make it hard for governments to resist granting licences for operations on even the most sensitive sites. Environmental risks during and well beyond operation include the production and disposal of both toxic and non-toxic waste, and the impact of mining on water supplies to the local environment. Following initial investment, a mine may remain in operation for several decades, possibly including lengthy periods of inactivity, before permanently ceasing production. During that period ownership of the mine may change many times, especially as it nears the end of life, when potential future liabilities begin to outstrip likely short term profits. Mines close to closure have even been given to the local community, but not accompanied by the resources to undertake restitution of the site. The issue of who is to be held liable, and how that liability should be enforced, both for the general making good of a closed site and for dealing with any specific unexpected events such as dam failures, is not easy to determine. Meanwhile, changes in government or government policy may have led to state controlled money previously taken from revenues and taxes, to be earmarked for legacy issues, being diverted to other causes.

5. Social and economic concerns were a particular feature of the conversations we undertook with local communities. We heard much about what is often referred to as the "Resource Curse", whereby the discovery and extraction of natural resources can leave both the local community, and sometimes the wider nation, worse off. The often complex relationships between different companies within an international group structure leave lots of scope for pricing decisions that allow profits to land in whichever jurisdiction is most favourable to parent body. This is not specific to extraction, as large data companies operate similar structures. But the unique aspect of extraction is that it is a "one time only" business. Once natural resources have been exhausted, they are gone.

Because mining products are traded globally, they are subject to the high levels of volatility in the commodity markets. Small differences in supply and demand can lead to massive swings in prices, as we saw on a visit to a platinum mine. When the price is low, operations can be put on hold awaiting an upswing. This can lead to workers being laid off for long and indeterminate periods. It can also dry up the revenue streams that both the local and national government relies on to sustain the wider economy and achieve development goals. Where mining activities have led to a significant growth in local population, closure can then result in high levels of unemployment among a workforce that has long lost connection to the places from which it originally migrated. On our site visits we saw some good examples of mining companies investing in training workers for future careers other than mining, and of companies investing in the education of children for wider employment. However, such examples were far from universal.

Mines often require far more workers than the settled local population can provide, hence facilities for temporary migrant workers are a common feature. On some sites, accommodation arrangements, based on large dormitories with only very basic facilities, leave much to be desired. However, where management make efforts to upgrade accommodation, for example including provision for workers to bring their families, these can be shunned by workers desperate to minimise expenditure in order to send as much money as possible to support their families and dependents. Where workers lodge in overcrowded conditions, they create environments highly conducive to the spread of diseases such as AIDS and other sexually transmitted conditions, as well as making it far harder to sustain healthy relationships with their families and dependents, resident far away.

Issues for further sector-wide action

Many of the issues discussed above are ones that emerge, sometimes at short notice, in particular locations. They require church investors to have access to good monitoring systems, both through ESG agencies and via church networks and aid bodies. They can then have intensive engagement at company level, with the possibility of divestment in the event of insufficient progress being made. However, some represent sector-wide concerns, and the study concluded that follow-up work might explore Joint Ventures, protected areas – and tailings dams.

Joint Ventures are a normal part of global business. They allow partners to work together, bringing their different skills and strengths, to respond to a specific opportunity. In particular, a mining company may well seek a partner with local knowledge and local connections, in order to gain the best understanding of the local community, and the regulatory and political environment, in which it will be operating.

Extractive Industries – A Case Study on Investor Engagement

However, the use of such special purpose vehicles can serve to dilute standards, whilst mitigating the liability and reputational risk consequent on poor controls. Moreover international operators may be required to work with local partners whose main characteristic is closeness to the governing regime or presidential family, and whose principal objective is the generation of private wealth for those individuals.

The search for economically extractable commodities ranges ever wider and, as technology advances, more remote and sensitive locations can become increasingly attractive. Oil exploration in the Arctic has been perhaps the most politically high profile example in recent years. When a group of environmental campaigners invaded the Edinburgh headquarters of an exploration company dressed as polar bears, they were drawing attention to the high environmental risks incurred even before commercial extraction might begin. Exploration companies are often small specialist operations, keeping the risks associated with cleaning up after spills in sensitive areas well away from the balance sheets of the bodies who would, were permission granted, eventually exploit the site. Campaigners have highlighted that the explorers carry nothing like the level of capital backing or insurance to cover a major incident, relying instead on simply allowing the company to go bankrupt and moving on. Whilst spills are an example of mining gone wrong, in other areas such as the Virunga Park (of which more later) the mere fact of any mining would destroy a vital and protected habitat, even if it was carried out to the best possible standards.

The new tailings dam standard

In January 2019, shortly after the EIAG advice was adopted by the National Investment Bodies, a tailings dam associated with an iron ore mine owned by a large international company, Vale, failed at Brumadinho in Brazil. The collapse of the dam released a sea of mud, which engulfed a populated area in its pathway, leading to 270 deaths and the destruction of much farmland. Less than four years earlier another dam, operated by a Vale subsidiary in the same state, had also collapsed with 19 fatalities and the destruction of two villages.

Given the scale of deaths, the Brumadinho tragedy featured in global news headlines for some days. This created a context in which multiple investors, mine owners and community representatives recognised the need to make a wider response. Armed with the newly

Extractive Industries – A Case Study on Investor Engagement

produced EIAG report, and building on the methodology adopted for the recently successful experience of forming the Transition Pathways Initiative as a multi-investor coalition on Climate Change, the National Investment Bodies were in a strong position to convene a sector wide partnership with the aim of producing new international standards for tailings that investors could urge companies to adopt.

On 5th August 2020, around 18 months later, and following intensive consultations, an event was convened from Church House, Westminster. This was the launch of the New Global Industry Standard on Tailings Management. It was jointly launched by UNEP (United Nations Environment Programme), ICMM (International Council on Mining and Metals - the principal trade body for the industry) and PRI (Principles for Responsible Investment - an investor partnership representing over 100 trillion dollars in assets under management). Adam Matthews of the Church of England Pensions Board, and one of the key drivers of the programme, represented PRI at the launch.

The Standard is detailed and comprehensive. It is divided into six topic areas covering: projected affected people; the social, environmental and economic context; quality of construction, operation and maintenance of dams through to closure; management and governance; emergency preparedness and response; public disclosure of information regarding dams. Members of ICMM have to commit to the Standard. It needs to be recognised that not all mine owners are ICMM members, particularly those resident in countries less interested in safety and good practice. However, the Council includes many of the larger and more investable institutions - those where shareholder pressure can most readily be brought to bear. The achievement in bringing such a diverse group of stakeholders to agree the Standard cannot be overestimated. As with the earlier example of Climate Change, it would appear that whilst the Church of England NIBs are far from the largest institutional investors, they carry considerable convening power and moral authority because of their association with the Church and also the existing reputation of the NIBs in the field of Ethical Investment.

Company specific exclusions

As we prepared to begin our work on extractives, we were particularly aware of permission having been granted for oil exploration in the Virunga National Park, a UNESCO World Heritage Site located in

Extractive Industries – A Case Study on Investor Engagement

the Democratic Republic of Congo. Operations would have placed a large proportion of the world's mountain gorillas at extreme risk. In 2013, the company involved, then known as SOCO international and registered in London, was made subject to intense engagement by the National Investment Bodies in order to obtain unequivocal assurances that the company would relinquish its operating permits and unconditionally withdraw. During conversations, it became clear that the company wished to retain its options, notwithstanding high profile criticism from the WWF. It had found support for reducing the park's boundaries among senior Congolese government figures, however international bodies, including UNESCO, were adamant that any such changes would viewed badly. Press reports at the time highlighted credible allegations of bribery and corruption, these alongside the refusal to unequivocally withdraw, and amid concerns that the company's directors were insufficiently independent, underpinned the July 2015 decision to sell the church's stake. By 2018 the company no longer had any African investments. In 2019, it changed its name to Pharos Energy.

Five years previously similar action was taken with regard to Vedanta Resources, but on different grounds. Vedanta had obtained permission to construct a large open cast mine on Niyamgiri mountain in the Orissa area of India. The mountain is held sacred by the local 8,000 strong Dongria Kondh tribe and development of the site risked destruction of the entire ecosystem. As would happen later with SOCO, engagement took place with the company, who proved unwilling to scrap their plans. As also with SOCO, the process of engagement raised concerns about the ability or willingness of non executive directors to provide robust governance in the face of executive resistance. After a series of high profile disinvestments by the Church and other shareholders, the Indian government itself took the lead, initiating a series of legal actions and a referendum of local people. This culminated in an Indian Supreme Court ruling in April 2016, confirming that the mine could not go ahead.

These stories illustrate that individual disinvestment is best kept as a very last resort. In neither case is it likely that the Church decision proved a determining factor in changing the views of the company. Public disinvestment by a church body is news for a day, but thereafter all opportunity to influence is lost. Church influence is much more effective when the strong ethical investment brand of the NIBs can be used to convene much wider coalitions of investors and allied parties.

This has already been convincingly demonstrated in terms of Climate Change via the Transition Pathways Initiative. It will be important to monitor the impact of the Tailing Dam Standard over the next few years, to see if it can create a similar industry-wide change of direction. Meanwhile the Ethical Investment Advisory Group has moved on to undertake a similar exploration of the world of big data.

David Walker is the Bishop of Manchester, Deputy Chair of the EIAG and Deputy Chair of the Church Commissioners' Board of Governors.

Monotheism as a foundation for ethics

JONATHAN CLATWORTHY

This article defends monotheism, understood as divine harmony, by contrasting the ethical implications with the divine conflict of many polytheisms and the atheist alternative. In divine conflict polytheism, humanity is characteristically threatened. Communities depend on a class of experts to appease the gods. This legitimates hierarchical, unequal societies. Divine harmony denies these threats and posits a supreme moral authority to whom the oppressed can appeal. Atheism excludes gods from public affairs, leaving the ruling classes as arbiters of public ethics. This recreates some of the unfortunate features of divine conflict polytheism.

This article defends monotheism as the most satisfactory foundation for ethics.[1] I contrast its ethical implications first with polytheism and then with atheism. Currently monotheism is unpopular:

> "The great unmentionable evil at the center of our culture is monotheism. From a barbaric Bronze Age text known as the Old Testament, three antihuman religions have evolved—Judaism, Christianity, and Islam. These are sky-god religions... Those who would reject him must be converted or killed for their own good. Ultimately, totalitarianism is the only sort of politics that can truly serve the sky-god's purpose... One God, one King, one Pope, one master in the factory, one father-leader in the family at home."[2]

Here Gore Vidal represented a generation of campaigners against the Cold War. Governments threatened nuclear annihilation in the name of defending western values against Communism.[3] In the USA those values were tightly wrapped up in the rhetoric of Christianity. Opponents rejected the god in whose name it was being threatened.

Monotheism has been compared unfavourably with polytheism

since the eighteenth century. To David Hume, 'the intolerance of almost all religions, which have maintained the unity of god, is as remarkable as the contrary principle in polytheists'.[4] Edward Gibbon 'turned his eyes from theological explanations and instead listed intolerance as the first of his famous five reasons for the triumph of Christianity'.[5]

Monotheism and polytheism

Whether those cold war claims really were monotheistic depends on one's definitions. The word 'monotheism' first appeared in the seventeenth century to distinguish it from 'polytheism', a word used by Philo in the first century CE to distinguish Judaism from it. Polytheism has often been described as an obvious response to human experience:

> "Polytheism is natural... It expresses the natural diversity of reality quite well, and enables people to cope with the individual numinous expressions of nature by making each one a god."[6]

Monotheism has been defined in many ways.[7] Here, to focus on the ethical implications, I distinguish it as belief in *divine harmony* as opposed to *divine conflict*. Theories of divine harmony see a unified divine authority as the supreme source of both moral authority and the way the universe operates. This contrasts with divine conflict theories where different transcendent powers have different moral stances and agendas.

Using this distinction, Christian doctrines like the Trinity and the divinity of Christ do not undermine monotheism except when they claim conflict between divine persons – for example, the Christian 'victory' theory of the Atonement, where the devil has real power over God.[8] Conversely, some polytheistic traditions in the ancient world gradually abandoned their theories of divine conflict and approximated to some kind of monotheism.[9]

Applying this distinction, the 'monotheist' propaganda of military aggressors, despite having echoed through the ages,[10] is not monotheistic at all. Recent discussions of ancient Assyrian beliefs illustrate the reason. Sargon II described how he united different nations in his empire 'to teach them how to fear God and the king'. The main word to characterise gods was *puluhtu*, fear.[11] Van de Mieroop summarises:

"The king, as representative of the god Assur, represented order. Wherever he was in control, there was peace, tranquility, and justice, and where he did not rule there was chaos. The king's duty to bring order to the entire world was the justification for military expansion. This idea pervaded royal rhetoric. All that was foreign was hostile, and all foreigners were like non-human creatures. Images of swamp-rats or bats, lonely, confused, and cowardly, were commonly applied to those outside the king's control."[12]

Some have described this as monotheism. The argument is that Assur was the maker and sovereign lord of the whole universe and thus transcendent. The connection with humans was established through the other gods, who were emanations of Assur. The other gods, therefore, were 'aspects or powers of a single universal God', a bit like the archangels of Jewish and Christian thought.[13]

However, divine harmony it was not. The military propaganda built a monotheistic veneer on top of a thoroughly polytheistic substance. The veneer is that there is one god of the whole world so there should be one king of the whole world. Anyone who resists the king's rule, whether inside or outside the empire, is resisting the supreme god and should be punished. This is the broadcast claim.

The polytheistic substance is characteristic of Mesopotamian cosmologies: the creation of the world is described in terms of battles between gods.[14] Logically, it does not follow that because there is one god of the world there should be one king of the world. The connection is exemplary rather than logical: the king should establish supremacy by defeating other kings just as the national god established supremacy by defeating other gods. Without those enemy gods the theological model would have been a peaceful one. Assyrian invaders sometimes made a point of destroying the images of foreign gods, believing that thereby they were depriving their enemies of divine protection – which of course implies that those enemy gods were real enough.[15]

Hence the contradiction. Internally it suited Assyrian kings to present other gods as totally subservient to Assur, just as they expected their human subjects to be subservient to them. For the purposes of warfare, on the other hand, there were enemy gods. In the same way, if at the height of the Cold War the dominant versions of American Christianity had been monotheistic, they would have recognised that God had no more wish to see bombs dropped on Russians than on Americans.

The theological contrast is often illustrated by comparing the creation story of ancient Babylon, the *Enuma Elish*, with the first chapter of Genesis – which may be partly a deliberate reaction against it.[16] In the Babylonian epic, after much fighting between the gods Marduk emerged supreme. To please the other gods he created humans to maintain temples and burn sacrifices. Floods, epidemics and military defeat were divine punishment for human failings like inadequate sacrifices. Eckart Otto describes the theology:

"In Mesopotamian tradition man was created from the blood of a god who represents chaos and guilt, and thus bears within himself elements of a life bound to failure. This negative anthropology is linked to a pessimistic idea of the aim of human life, whose purpose is to relieve gods who have become guilty of the burden of work."[17]

The sacrificial system was a form of taxation. A tablet from third century BCE Uruk has survived, listing the daily food requirements of the gods there. Their appetites were colossal: among the meat items were five whole sheep per god.[18] At least the priests must have known that those wooden statues did not actually eat anything; but the priests were the beneficiaries, backed up by the army. The rationale was that if the peasants did not provide what the gods demanded, the gods would punish the nation. This was a recipe for extreme economic exploitation. However hungry the peasants were, they had to give their best animals to the temple: it would be better for their children to starve to death than for the world order to revert to the original chaos.

The first chapter of Genesis, by contrast, stresses that the creation is good. Living beings are created as a blessing and encouraged to flourish. To Otto, Genesis 'is quite deliberate in providing a contrast: the one God had created humans to be partners and collaborators'.[19] John Barton summarises the ethical implications:

"Israelite ethics rests on an optimistic anthropology in which the human race is created as something good and is seen as capable of living in fellowship with God, whereas in Mesopotamia the creation of humans is an aspect of the chaotic in the world. The vision of Psalm 8 is not shared by other ancient Near Eastern cultures… [Israelite theology] inevitably leads to a different way of thinking about society and about moral norms, and leads to that stress on human solidarity which is inimical to the idea of domination by one person over others."[20]

Ethical implications

In the contrast between these two theological traditions we can see a consistency that produces their characteristic implications for the human condition. In the case of divine conflict they are these:

Order. The world order, both physical and moral, depends on events in the divine realm and is therefore to some extent provisional. Humanity has limited security, both because conflict between the gods may lead to a different world order and because the gods may change their plans.

Morality. The highest moral authorities are the gods, who characteristically make demands on humans – sometimes conflicting ones. They may also leave us to our own devices much of the time. The overall effect is moral relativism.

Purpose. Human life has been designed for non-human purposes. This provides a communal agenda for human activity. Between us we must work hard enough to meet the requirements. Essential to this agenda is discipline, and therefore hierarchy. At the top are the experts who know what needs to be done. At the bottom are those who fail to contribute adequately. They are dispensable. Suffering and starvation by dispensables is not a high priority.

Evil. The evils and suffering of the world result from divine activity. While this exonerates humanity from responsibility, it means there is nothing we can do about it. Life is, necessarily, tragic. Only the gods can do anything about it.

Divine harmony produces contrasting characteristics:

Order. The physical order has been securely established.[21] Whether human activity destroys the environment is of course another matter.

Morality. There is an ultimate moral truth, transcending all human values, built into the way things are.[22]

Purpose. The purpose of human life is fulfilment. The forces governing the world provide for our needs and do not threaten us. The communal agenda is to make sure everybody's needs are met. There may still be a role for experts, but there is no need for a hierarchical society. The well-being of everyone is a priority. When some go without the necessities of life, the cause lies with some taking more than their share. Lenn Goodman argues:

> "In a tribal society or primitive civilization where right is proportioned to power it might seem absurd to claim that the standing of the orphan, widow or stranger before law is and ought to be no less than that of the most powerful and prosperous citizen. From the standpoint of an absolute source of all values, their standing can be no less."[23]

Evil. Evil and suffering are not divinely caused. Some defenders of this view have minimised the element of evil;[24] others have appealed to the 'free will defence': that God gives humans freedom to choose between good and evil.[25]

Atheism

Using this model of the ethical differences, we can now ask how atheism compares. What if there are no gods, or if the gods are irrelevant? If there are no gods there is no moral authority above humans. All moral discourse is a product of humans. We create our own values. So why have any moral discourse at all? Is it all a big mistake inherited from our religious past?

Perhaps. Charles Stevenson's Ethics and Language, the classic statement of Emotivism, argued that each moral statement is a combination of a factual statement with an imperative. 'This is wrong' means 'I disapprove of this; do so as well'. All moral talk, he concluded, is really nothing but psychological manipulation.[26] Since then a number of ethicists have argued that this is the way popular discourse actually treats moral controversies today.[27]

Most secular ethicists seek to be more constructive. In practice every society needs moral norms to guide its members. There are two tasks. One is to establish which moral norms should be applied. The other is to produce a theory explaining why they should be obeyed.

The current range of theories is often summarised as 'rights, duties and goals': judging the morality of actions according to human rights, or rational accounts of autonomous morality, or predictions of consequences.

There is one weakness which all such theories share in their secular form. To illustrate it I shall refer to John Rawls' *A Theory of Justice*, arguably the most influential work of ethics since the Second

World War.

Rawls developed a modernised version of social contract theory which, he argued, could lead to agreement on the values a society should have. It is based on a thought experiment. We are to imagine that we are all behind a 'veil of ignorance', not knowing which role we will play in real life. In this situation, he argued, we would vote for an egalitarian society. From this he concluded that a relatively egalitarian society is what we should aim for. He allowed an element of inequality but only to the extent that it benefited the least advantaged. [28]

Critics complained either of its individualism – presupposing self-centred individuals negotiating against each other for personal advantage – or that we are not behind a veil of ignorance, we know what we have got, and some would rather keep it this way. In his later writings Rawls accepted that his theory did not have universal application:

> "Justice as Fairness presents itself not as a conception of justice which is true; but one that can serve as a basis of informed and willing agreement between citizens viewed as free and equal persons."[29]

Critics then argued that this undermines his earlier claims." John Gray responded:

> "Rawls takes as his point of departure, not a general theory of human nature, but what he calls 'the public culture of a democratic society' – roughly speaking the intuitions common among American East Coast liberal academics. The upshot of his theorizing is not a political conception of general human interest, but an apology for American institutions."[30]

Of course it is. If the only moral norms are the ones any society creates for itself, Rawls could have done no other. Here lies a weakness of all secular attempts at ethical theories. There are two aspects. The first is that, whereas theological theories seek to discover the moral norms by which God has designed us to live, secular theories seek to create norms. If so, it can only create them for non-moral reasons – because until it has created them it has no basis for making moral judgements. Even after it has created them, there remains the issue of whether it is justified in coercing its members to obey them. Inevitably, when rulers and intellectuals consider themselves competent to create an ethical system for their society, it will protect their own interests.

The second aspect is that, in the absence of any moral truths that transcend all humans, whatever any moral philosopher proposes is only their proposal. It will always be open to others to prefer a different one. The matter boils down to nothing more than personal preference, like choosing between strawberries and raspberries. Experience tells us that humanity is far too diverse for any one proposal to get unanimous support.

Atheist presuppositions

With this in mind it should now be possible to compare the relevant features of atheism with divine harmony and divine conflict.

Order. The universe is maintained by unthinking, determined laws of nature that do not decide anything at all, let alone care about humans. This locates atheism closer to polytheism, where the gods have limited concern for humans, than to monotheism – but takes it to an extreme. For all we know a meteor will destroy our planet next year, or climate change was about to wipe us out anyway.

Morality. In the absence of any transcendent moral authorities we humans create our own values. In practice the dominant values are those of the ruling classes and controllers of the mass media. Like those Mesopotamian gods they care more for their own interests than for other humans, and they are also in constant dispute with each other. Morality is relative, and perhaps means no more than emotional manipulation.

Purpose. In principle, human life has no purpose at all. In practice, countries with secular constitutions nearly always operate with a strong sense of communal purpose. Government rhetoric emphasises the priority of managing the economy. Market forces, in a limited world where we cannot all have our own refrigerator, computer and motor car, are depicted as a tragic feature of the way things are. Government after government postpones expenditure on those in most need until 'we have got the economy moving again'. Thus, in the absence of a transcendent purpose, the ruling classes present themselves as our leaders in a communal agenda of struggling against the tragic nature of reality. Once again we depend on experts and must do what they tell us, however hard they make us work. The polarisation of wealth, which has been increasing for over forty years across the industrialised

West, has produced an ever-steeper hierarchy of power. We now have a growing number of homeless people, illustrating society's willingness to discard those who do not contribute to the communal agenda. Naomi Klein cites a survey of new USA college students. In 1966, 44% said that making a lot of money was 'very important' or 'essential'. In 2013 the percentage had jumped to 82%. [31]

Evil. National well-being suffers from shortage of resources. This has been a central presupposition of capitalist economic theory since the eighteenth century. Once again humanity is exonerated from responsibility. Life is, necessarily, tragic. The hope of future improvement is more positive than it was for ancient polytheists but it is still based on the communal agenda, now dominated by economic growth and technological innovation.

Conclusion

I have described three alternative theories of the human condition and their ethical implications. Comparing the elements has involved much generalisation but the overall pattern is clear. Monotheism is the odd one out. In the other two, the world order is less secure; morality is relative; a communal agenda requires hard work supervised by a powerful elite in a hierarchical society relegating many to destitution; and the conditions of human life are fundamentally tragic. Atheism offers more hope of future improvement than does divine conflict, but in every other instance its distance from monotheism is greater.

We might therefore think of atheist accounts of the human condition as a successor to polytheism. This leaves us with two options. To a large extent they represent the left/right debates of modern politics.

On one side, the disappointments of human experience are caused by the physical world order. This justifies an agenda of economic and technological change managed by the ruling classes, and demands hard work and an unequal society.

On the other side, the disappointments of human experience are not caused by the physical world order. They are caused by the failure of humans to care for each other. Here the ethical norms are egalitarian: what matters is to make sure everybody's needs are met.

It is easy to see why monotheism appeals to the impoverished and oppressed. By offering them a moral authority that transcends the ruling classes, it gives them a worldview from which to denounce their oppressors. We do not need to fatalistically shrug our shoulders at evil and suffering; we can do something about it. Conversely, most governments dislike it: they prefer to believe that everything wrong with their society is caused by tragic forces beyond their control. It is not surprising that the monotheism which first created Judaism, Christianity and Islam has in each case been watered down over time.

Yet the two are not on a par. Atheists consider themselves entitled to disagree with their governments. Every time they do, they appeal to a moral authority higher than humans. In practice our society, for all its apparent secularism, is riddled with appeals to transcendent moral authorities. We no longer call them gods. We call them by other names, like human rights or the sanctity of life, and we have learned not to examine what on earth we mean by them. But we believe they are there, guiding us in how we should live. We cannot do without some act of trust in harmonious, benign and reliable transcendence. If we could reflect on it more realistically we might acquire a better understanding of how to live well in this world we have been given.

Jonathan Clatworthy is a trustee of Modern Church, blogger and author. His most recent book is Why Progressives Need God.

Notes

1. This is an edited version of the talk given at the 'Modern Church' conference in July 2017. It summarises the thesis of Clatworthy, Jonathan, *Why Progressives Need God*, Alresford: Christian Alternative, 2017.
2. Gore Vidal, 'Monotheism' in *Selected Essays of Gore Vidal*, New York: Doubleday, 2008. pp. 410-11. This essay was the Harvard University Lowell Lecture in 1992.
3 Carter Heyward, *The Redemption of God: A Theology of Mutual Relation*, Washington DC: UP of America, 1982; Daphne Hampson, *After Christianity*, London: SCM, 1996; Mary Daly, *Beyond God the Father: Towards a Philosophy of Women's Liberation,* London: Women's Press, 1985; Rodney Stark, *For the Glory of God: How Monotheism led to Reformations, Science, Witch-Hunts, and the End of Slavery*, Princeton: Princeton University Press, 2003; Stark, *One True God: Historical Consequences of Monotheism*, Princeton: Princeton UP, 2001; Rosemary Radford Ruether, *Sexism and God-Talk,* London: SCM, 1983; Sharon D Welch, *A Feminist Ethic of Risk*, Minneapolis: Fortress, 1990; Allan S

Mohl, 'Monotheism: its influence on patriarchy & misogyny', *Journal of Psychohistory*, Summer 2015, Vol 43, Issue 2.
4. Hume, *Natural History of Religion*, 9,20.
5. H A Drake, 'Monotheism and violence', *Journal of Late Antiquity*, Vol 6, Issue 2, 2013, p. 251.
6. Robert Karl Gnuse, *No Other Gods: Emergent Monotheism in Israel*, Sheffield: Sheffield Academic Press, 1997, p. 215.
7. C. Frevel provides a list in 'Beyond monotheism? Some remarks and questions on conceptualising "monotheism" in biblical studies', *Verbum et Ecclesia* 34(2), Art. #810.
8. Aulén, Gustaf, *Christus Victor: An Historical Study of the Three Main Types of the Idea of the Atonement*, London: SPCK, 1931. Conflict with the devil is dualistic rather than polytheistic, but the ethical effect is still conflict within the divine realm.
9. Polymnia Athanassiadi, *Pagan Monotheism In Late Antiquity*, Oxford: Clarendon, 1999.
10. 'The defining characteristic of late antiquity... was its conviction that knowledge of the One God both justifies the exercise of imperial power and makes it more effective. Antecedents of this idea can be traced in the polytheist world of ancient Greece and Rome, but Constantine placed it at the center of Roman political ideology when he became a Christian.' Garth Fowden, *From Empire to Commonwealth: Consequences of Monotheism in Late Antiquity*, Princeton: Princeton UP, 1993, p. 3. Similarly Genghis Khan is reputed to have said: 'In heaven there is no-one but the one God alone; on earth no-one but the one ruler Genghis Khan'. Gnuse, *No Other Gods*, p. 148.
11. Walter Burkert, *Creation of the Sacred: Tracks of Biology in Early Religions*, Cambridge, Mass: Harvard UP, 1996, pp. 31, 93-95.
12. Marc Van De Mieroop, *A History of the Ancient Near East*, Oxford: Blackwell, 2004, p. 243.
13. Parpola, 'Monotheism', in Barbara Nevling Porter, Ed, *One God or Many? Concepts of Divinity in the Ancient World*, Chebeague, Maine: Casco Bay Assyriological Institute, 2000, pp. 165-80. The claim is debated: see Barbara Porter, ibid, pp. 214-5 and 235-237,
14. Jean Bottéro, *Religion in Ancient Mesopotamia*, Chicago: Uni Chicago Press, 2001; H W F Saggs, *The Encounter with the Divine in Mesopotamia and Israel*, London: Athlone, 1978.
15. Gerald Janzen, 'On the Moral Nature of God's Power: Yahweh and the Sea in Job and Deutero-Isaiah', *Catholic Biblical Quarterly* 56, '1994, p. 461; Jan Assmann, *Of God and Gods: Egypt, Israel, and the Rise*

of Monotheism, London: University of Sisconsin Press, 2008, p. 30.
16. Mark Smith, *The Priestly Vision of Genesis 1*, Minneapolis: Fortress, 2010.
17. Eckart Otto, quoted in John Barton, *Understanding Old Testament Ethics*, London: Westminster John Knox Press, 2003, p. 1.
18. Jean Bottéro, *Religion in Ancient Mesopotamia*, Chicago: Uni Chicago Press, 2001, p. 128.
19. Quoted in Barton, *Understanding*, p. 1. See also Eckart Otto, 'Law and Ethics', in Sarah Iles Johnston, *Religions of the Ancient World: A Guide*, Cambridge, MA & London: Harvard UP, 2004, pp. 87-89.
20. Barton, *Understanding*, pp. 168-169.
21. While Hume and Gibbon praised polytheism for its tolerance they took for granted the real potential of modern science, made possible by monotheism's confidence in the regularities of nature. Divine conflict theology could not have justified any confidence in regular laws of nature.
22. Whether it can be reduced to a set of moral rules is a different question. However it does avoid the 'Euthyphro dilemma'. Plato's Euthyphro asks why it is right to obey the gods: simply because the gods so command, or because their commands are right anyway? Secular ethicists argue that In the former case the gods' commands are arbitrary and in the latter the gods are irrelevant. In monotheism this dilemma does not arise because the source of moral commands is also the source of the physical universe: to obey God is to follow the maker's instructions.
23. Lenn Evan Goodman, *Monotheism: A Philosophical Inquiry Into the Foundations of Theology and Ethics*, Totowa, New Jersey: Allanheld, Osmun, 1981, p. 94.
24. E.g. Matthew Fox, *Original Blessing*, Santa Fé, New Mexico: Bear & Co, 1983.
25. The best known defence of this is John Hick, *Evil And the God of Love*, London: Collins, 1974. In my *Why Progressives Need God* I argue that the second and third chapters of Genesis can be read as a theodicy of this type, responding to the otherwise all-controlling God of Genesis 1.
26. Charles L Stevenson, *Ethics and Language*, New Haven: Yale University Press, 1944, pp. 21-26, 54-60.
27. E.g. Alasdair MacIntyre, *After Virtue: A Study in Moral Theory*, London: Duckworth, 1985, Chapter 2.
28. John Rawls, *A Theory of Justice*, Oxford: OUP, 1973.

29. 'Justice as fairness: political not metaphysical', Philosophy and Public Affairs, 1985, 14, quoted by Maureen Ramsay, *What's Wrong with Liberalism?*, London: Leicester University Press, 1997, p. 230.
30. John Gray, *Endgames: Questions in late modern political thought*, Oxford: Blackwell, 1997, p. 53. Similarly Ramsay responds that 'it is rather an odd defence of liberal principles of justice to say that they are liberal principles of justice; to say that people conceived the way liberals conceive them would choose liberal principles; to say that a liberal theory of justice informed by liberal beliefs and values is one that liberals could accept' (Ramsay, Liberalism, p. 124).
31. Naomi Klein, *This Changes Everything*, London: Penguin, 2015, p. 60.

Forum

Churches and the pandemic

Rob Marshall

*'I was glad when they said unto me
Let's take note and do things differently?'*

Risk Averse

The COVID-19 pandemic, and everything that ensues from it, is leading to the re-evaluation and re-assessment of many aspects of pre-pandemic life. The churches of course are not exempt from this.

First, however, let us review a major decision in England, replicated in the rest of the UK, which affected places of worship at an early stage of the pandemic. The March 2020 declaration from the archbishops of Canterbury and York determined that "Our church buildings must now be closed not only for public worship, but for private prayer as well, and this includes priests or lay persons offering prayer in church on their own."[1] A pandemic was raging. Hospitalisations and deaths were rising. But the locking out of religious leaders from buildings for which they were responsible, even if they were to be temporarily closed to the public, caused both unrest and confusion amongst church leaders. This later led to increasing anger and frustration.

The virus began to make its effects felt in the UK in late February/early March 2020. Deserted streets, the isolation of family groups and a cessation of normal work and leisure activity all contributed to a feeling of fear and uncertainty. It was a truly awful disease from which millions of people around the world have perished without warning. Many families, my own included, were touched by death and tragedy. Their passing became part of a narrative of despair and confusion.

Globally, the healthcare sector was placed under immense pressure. Children were prevented from going to school and students to college or university. Pubs, cafes and restaurants were mothballed. There was a cultural earthquake during which the performing arts and many sports were decimated. There was early talk of the devastating consequences for the nation's mental health as people wrestled with multiple hurdles in their lives as face-coverings finally became compulsory. We were placed in confinement [the French word for lockdown] and sealed in.

Which is why the March 2020 announcement re churches was, in hindsight, so very wrong. Closing churches for public worship was understandable in the circumstances. But community-based faith leaders [clergy and laity] were to be also prevented from entering their buildings even to pray. The inability of clergy to pray for their people in situ and to be seen online celebrating the sacraments and leading worship in local churches in tandem with the extraordinary embracing of modern technology which materialised almost overnight, was a regrettable move.

The kind of inert disappointment felt by many clergy of all denominations was summed up well by Serenhed James in *The Critic* a few weeks later:

> "The rhythm of prayer offered in the parish churches remains a quiet, gentle, heartbeat in a storm of nationwide noise. Moreover, for many clergy—and especially for those on the Catholic wing of the Church of England, who tend also to serve in some of the grittiest places—to celebrate the Eucharist daily at the altars of their churches is not some sort of treat to be enjoyed when conditions allow, but the *fons et origo* of their lives as priests, from which they draw the inner strength that sustains a life of outward service."

More recently, Welby has conceded that it was a mistake to prevent clergy from entering their churches for that oddly described activity - "private prayer". He had, he said, been too risk averse.[2] *The Church Times*' coverage of the online July 2020 General Synod meeting, and the questions to the Archbishop, makes for uncomfortable reading. This was the first time Welby had been called to public account for his actions. Indeed, the report suggests he received a "grilling". It resulted in a "testy" archbishop and it was uncomfortable to watch: "Everyone was at the end of their tether, trying to work very rapidly.... that was why we were not able to deal with the legal side. We were under enormous pressure," he told Synod members.

Dr Edward Dowler, Archdeacon of Hastings, was one of several leading voices to question of the legality of the decision. He pleaded

"Let the clergy pray in their churches" and reminded his readers of Psalm 122.1: "I was glad when they said unto me: we will go into the House of the Lord." He added: "The response to this required a targeted research-led approach to risk rather than further restrictions added to an already unprecedented limitation of social freedom in this country".[3]

I avoid suggesting that this action resulted in a missed opportunity because this would imply the taking advantage of the horrendous suffering and death that many witnessed. But at the very moment communities stuck at home really needed to know that their priests and ministers were praying with them in familiar sacred spaces, for the transfiguration of despair into glory, the lights were tuned off and the ecclesiastical doors were locked. How were the churches going to respond when the red light went amber?

Blinking into a new liturgical landscape

There was no one day when the churches re-opened. It happened over a period of time. Several factors determined the pace of re-opening. The capacity of the building to allow for social distancing was one factor. But there were other issues too including the non-availability of some clergy who had had to self-isolate on health grounds and were rightly cautious about resuming liturgical duties. Whilst the doors had been locked, however, a quiet technological revolution had begun, resulting in a learning curve for clergy that was so steep that it has left innumerable questions in its wake.

I now seek to address these questions in the remainder of this article. Simply in order to keep in touch and communicate with their local communities, churches did what many other parallel sectors such as education and business had to do. Churches had to discover, quickly and efficiently, methods of communicating the Gospel in new and challenging digital ways.

On one day, I had never heard of Zoom, but by the next it had become my administrative salvation. I knew that it was possible to broadcast on Facebook but was unaware of how simple it was. Once online, I had to learn quickly why the mute button suddenly became the most important thing in leading worship! But there was a plethora of new and urgent questions to consider:
- How to lead the daily offices and which platform suited best?
- What music can be used without copyright problems?
- How do we get the words of liturgy and hymns to the faithful?

Here, St Martin in the Fields were exemplary in providing pre-recorded seasonal hymns to parishes every week. Many of us are eternally grateful.
- What about Compline, parish meeting and school assemblies?
- Online purchases of tripods, microphones, tablets and phone rocketed. What were the best ones to buy?

Key Questions faced by most churches
- Who in the community has the technological know-how?
- What level of broadband is available if at all (difficult in more rural areas)?
- The realisation of the availability of otherwise unknown meeting platforms such as Zoom and Teams.
- Safeguarding and the prevention of unwanted intruders and inappropriateness in worship.
- Decisions on what to do with the main subcategories of worship:
- Eucharistic celebration
- Non eucharistic services
- Daily Offices including Morning and Evening Prayer and Compline
- Red letter days and festivals – making special provision
- Providing adequate help and support to local schools
- The key question of music as above.

Sociological Factors
There were three main subgroups of potential end-users/recipients for these communications:
- The connected and active
- The connected but disinterested
- The disconnected

The first group is obvious. The second group had the capacity to tune in and interact but with everything else going on, were unlikely to do so except on special occasions. The third group were a huge concern as they were often, in every way, the most isolated.

What was also immediately noticeable was clearly a surprise to many clergy and lay leaders. Despite the efforts of the national church and dioceses to step up the provision of online resources [the broadcasting of a Sunday service for instance] it soon became clear that worshippers wanted to remain connected and to support their local church. Being visible or heard locally was what really seemed to help people at the height of the pandemic. Because of my own background in radio we moved services to being largely audio-type offerings with many local voices taking part. Some weekends we would average 100+ listeners with interaction and responses as key. Other parishes went for the live streaming model which also worked for them – with an emphasis on the visual transmission. Local ruled.

Having been closed for many weeks, it was obvious that many would not return to church for a long time and, at the time of writing in October 2021, many still have not returned. They still tune in and rely on digital offerings either exclusively or alongside a rare, cautious visit to church. It was also clear that not all parishes had been able to respond, and some had felt bereft and left behind. It was obvious that whilst one parish had flourished, and adapted, others had been largely silent. For some clergy the technology was simply beyond them, or they were unwell, or they did not have a suitably tech-savvy back up team of laity to offer support.

The Bishop of Manchester, Dr David Walker, was candid enough to suggest that like many of the consequences of COVID-19, the disease would hasten key decisions about the long-term viability of churches which had already been hanging by a thread:

> "If I had a list of what sort of church is the one that's most likely to require closure, I'd be thinking typically of a mid-Victorian building that was built to last a century... But the physical structure is tired, it is very large, and there isn't the community around it that there was when it was built ... They were built to serve populations that just don't exist [now]."[4]

Mixed Economy Church

It is worth noting here that data from 12,700 churches analysed by the Church of England's Research and Statistics Unit[5] underlines the central tenet of my basic argument below that first, there is no going back; second, we have to act quickly to evaluate where we go next; and third, that structural change at diocesan level, or its equivalent in another denomination, is more critical than many in leadership positions seem to realise (they are also tired and disorientated as leaders).

Here is a summary of that data:
- 9000 churches switched at very short notice to offering online worship
- 8000 offered pre-recorded services
- 5000 offered downloadable services
- 2000 offered telephone or dial in services

The majority were still offering these after lockdown had ended, as many still are. Generally rural churches have done as well as urban churches.

To sum up where this leaves many churches as they continue to wrestle with the effects of the COVID-19 pandemic in terms of community engagement, liturgical offering and Christian nurture, I would offer the following ten observations.

Ten Key Points for ongoing reflection

1. Lobby for radical post-pandemic structural change

As far as the Church of England is concerned, the current synodical and diocesan structures including budgets, deployment and episcopal oversight are clearly not fit for purpose. My engagement with my own Diocese of St Albans reveals a superb effort on the part of the Diocesan Bishop and senior team to respond to the pandemic. At the same time, however, as the Bishop of Manchester observes, decisions that might have taken ten years to arrive at need to be taken now, in terms of the national, regional and local roll-out of resources, always bearing in mind that people seem to respond best to what is local.

2. What to do with the disconnected

This is a critical point. Every church knows that there remains a remnant of people who are disconnected and out of touch. We should not contemplate losing them or writing them off, and although they represent the tail end of a generation for whom a smart phone is anathema and the internet a non-starter, they have often given decades of service and have now lived through a time of terrible isolation and disorientation. They must not be forgotten.

3. How to define church membership

It is now more difficult to define what constitutes membership in a local church. There is a combination of core, involved members; then

Forum

there is the tangential group who dip in and out; next there are the unconnected who rely on telephone, post and physical visits. Another group is the pastoral contact group through occasional offices and other outreach, but how can these be categorised? Finally there are the digital members who interact solely with a church online. Thus in our parish we now have members in both Bristol and Doncaster who support the parish in Hertfordshire. This is a conscious choice, and they join us online and contribute to our work. In secular terms they have become fully paid-up members. It is a new phenomenon and they appear in no traditional assessment as attendees or members,

4. Focus on young people and schools
One of the major casualties of the pandemic for many churches was the lack of interaction with children, families, young people and schools. One obvious reason for this was that many children and young people found that their school learning had moved online and, therefore, any kind of church activity could too easily become an extension of online learning. In my own ministry I interact with at least seven schools varying from a pre-school nursery of children up to 18-year-old sixth formers. After a few months the regular recording of assemblies and online services did become difficult and challenging, as well as important.

5. Radical reappraisal of baptisms, weddings and funerals
Many clergy found that officiating at limited attendance funerals was a huge challenge. Many of these were also live streamed to those unable to travel or attend. Organising the funeral of my own father, who died at Christmas 2020, was hugely challenging, not least having to take paperwork to prove that staying at a hotel 200 miles away to be at his bedside was both possible and allowed.

Baptism and wedding families had interminable waits. Many of the children we baptised during the summer of 2021 were 2 or 3 years old. Their baptisms had been booked when some were just a few weeks old. Adapting the service to be more appropriate and yet still adhere to limitations such as social distancing was a challenge. But it was possible to detect a real sense of joy and relief that we could at last meet again. How we engage with such families in the future is now under real review.

6. The importance of ongoing local digital provision which speaks of Christian mindfulness

The Church of England research mentioned earlier referred to an ongoing need for online worship provision, even now that physical services can take place. This is obviously because many people engaging with local church offerings have become used to watching/listening to a service at a time that suits them. In my own parish, for example, we provide a specially recorded Compline service twice a week which uses the readings specific for that day, with live and pertinent intercessions. If this was to be held only in church, we might achieve 4/5 people maximum and fewer in winter. These audio offerings regularly attract 20+ people each time they are broadcast.

We used to have 4/5 people in church for Morning Prayer on a weekday. We now average 16 at the same service via Zoom. If we were to cease the Zoom offering those attending (some of them elderly) would not be able to take part. For the younger folk, there is no attraction to setting off to church in the middle of a school run when it can easily be done online. Avoiding unnecessary travel can help the environment but there is also the importance of physical social gatherings and seeing each other. How do we achieve this balance?

7. *A radical overview of the Christian year*
The mixed economy demands that local churches have an overview of the annual Christian year and the offering made to the community they serve in terms of online/physical events, service and interaction, across the whole age range.

8. *Embracing social media to effect communication and linkage*
Whenever a church offers a mixed economy of services, events and interaction, it must be backed up with a social media strategy which embraces the same offering. This is a new factor for many churches. The use of Facebook, Instagram and Twitter alongside the invaluable resource A Church Near You demands up to date and accurate copy which speaks to the whole community. This with our limited resources is a huge challenge.

9. *Transformation of administration*
One of the clearest advantages of online platforms for meetings is the ability of many church meetings and groups to be held online. Questions about the balance between seeing each other in person and avoiding extra time and travel need a new strategy for different post-COVID categories of meeting. It's clearly not Ideal for some attendees

to be in the room and others online. So this will take time to work out and to settle down. At the moment there is 'meeting tension' all around us.

10. Be upfront about stewardship and giving
Like every other aspect of our lives, churches have found themselves having to rethink methods of giving. Many people have adapted and moved their giving online. The open plate collection has become largely a thing of the past. People at special services are beginning to use their phone to make a donation where the technology is available locally. But let us not forget the importance of stewardship and giving. However generous people want to be, there needs to be an accepted methodology of giving. And it is often the same group of 'the disconnected' who used to bring their envelope to church every week and who are now thwarted by the challenge of online giving and banking.

Conclusion

The pandemic sneaked up on us. The churches were as ill-prepared as the rest of society. Some early decisions made in haste were clearly ill-advised. But laity and clergy rallied around, and research reveals how well the vast majority of churches did in responding to the challenge of digitalisation. Once they were able to re-open, it was immediately clear that there was no swift return to the old ways of doing things. Even going to church was a completely different experience. Seating, singing, sharing the sacraments – all had changed. But it was also clear that many of the innovations of the pandemic period had brought about transformation and change.

In many cases this was for the common good. The Gospel is finding new ways of being heard and shared. A 'mixed economy' – a term often used with regard to Fresh Expressions – is the way forward. This means not losing the essence of what it means to be ekklesia, but also not being blinkered to modern communications methodology and the adaptability of all age groups to learn and take part.

Vision, leadership and strategy are now needed: to embrace the church cultures of both pre- and post-pandemic times, and to forge a way forward so that churches are seen as both relevant and dynamic. And there are many positive signs of change indeed, as we survey the scenes of 'life after a pandemic' all around us.

The Revd Dr Rob Marshall is a writer and broadcaster, and Rector of Digswell, Welwyn Garden City. He has presented Pause for Thought and Thought for the Day on BBC Radio for more than 30 years.

Notes

1. https://thecritic.co.uk/priests-and-palaces/
2. *Christian Today*, 9 April 2021 reporting an interview Welby did with the Financial Times.
3. Edward Dowler 'Let the Clergy pray in their churches' [Church Times 31 March 2020]
4. https://www.theguardian.com/world/2021/jan/05/c-of-e-bishop-warns-of-church-closures-due-to-covid-financial-losses
5. https://www.churchofengland.org/media-and-news/press-releases/thousands-churches-offered-remote-worship-during-lockdown-new-report

Book Reviews

Christian Pacifism for an Environmental Age
Mark Douglas
Cambridge University Press, 2019, 269pp, hbk, £75

Blessed are the Peacemakers: Pacifism, Just War, and Peacebuilding
Lisa Sowle Cahill
Fortress Press, 2019, 380pp, pbk, £19.99

What joins these two excellent books is a sustained and serious effort to reinterpret two approaches to social ethics in Christian tradition: pacifism and 'peacebuilding'. Both volumes are strongly marked by present concerns: environmental issues and violence and war in a global context. They come to slightly different judgements on pacifism but both are broadly based, carefully argued, and—above all and emphatically to be welcomed—constructive.

In Christian Pacifism for an Environmental Age, Mark Douglas is concerned to rehabilitate Christian pacifism but not in the usual way and not against common objections. Moreover, any effort to reconsider pacifism now takes place in a context in which it has secured a certain pre-eminence, especially in North America. The Christian ethics of Martin Luther King and Stanley Hauerwas are widely discussed and there has been recently renewed attention to ethics in the Anabaptist tradition. Douglas' argument is not therefore an act of retrieval but more a work of retelling. The broad narrative in which pacifism is located needs revision, he argues, and thereafter he turns to Christian pacifism for an environmental age. The central theological issue he maintains is 'time': the passage through time of the Christian pacifist movement to when we are now living (2-3). To answer this question more adequately from the perspective Christian pacifism, a fresh telling is required.

What needs fixing in the standard telling, according to Douglas? The standard periodisation—the early Church was pacifist, but the adoption of Christianity by Constantine and then the just war ethics of Augustine displace the pacifist option until the Reformation and thereafter the option renews in the twentieth century with its wars and other violence—needs retelling in much less discontinuous fashion. Core to this retelling, according to Douglas, is making the pacifist witness less dominant and more varied before Constantine and more available as an option after Constantine; and overcoming the temptation to ascribe to early Christian pacifism a purity that for Douglas inhibits us from taking it up as a serious option. As Douglas makes clear, some organising principle of Eden/Fall/return to Eden seems to be operating here (or maybe an interrupted golden thread account of Christian social ethics?).

Yet this is not all the book's ambition. In addition, Douglas presents environmental issues, especially a warming climate, and their impact on issues of war and peace, as a fresh perspective on the pacificist tradition. This new perspective will require the development of the pacifist tradition. Moreover, Douglas argues than in their variety pacifist traditions are well placed to respond to the rigours of the twenty-first century. As he claims, '...both premodern and modern pacifists have largely ignored the impact of the natural world in shaping the conditions that led to violence...[and] are seeking more capacious language, more developed practices...as they rediscover their connections to the rest of creation' (214). Although there is at the conclusion a strong emphasis on peace and order, there is less detail on how we are to understand creaturely connections despite a highly interesting discussion of possible relations between violence and climate change (230-39).

At one point, Douglas suggests that religion scholars do not think across the topics of environment, war and peace, and religion (20). Lisa Sowle Cahill is a partial exception to that rule in that she notes the relationship between war and security issues, the poor, and climate change (ix). Claiming that Blessed are the Peace Makers is a reworking of her earlier Love your Enemies: Discipleship, Pacifism, and Just War Theory (1994)—which Douglas cites—Cahill proposes peacebuilding as a different way of characterising Christian responsibility other than the approaches of pacifism and just war. What, in Cahill's view, are the differences between her 1994 and 2019 arguments? First, that although she maintains her commitment to the primacy of pacifism she is more amenable to the claim that just war theory relates properly to ecclesial identity and evangelical political responsibility. Second, that thinking Christianly in this area often means facing 'irreducible moral dilemma[s]' and therefore appropriate responses should be governed less by the contrast between pacifism and just war and instead focus on peacebuilding 'which is not quandary free either, but

Book Reviews

it is a theological-practical approach, a creative living-out of Christian and ecclesial identity...' (xi).

The bulk of the book is a set of historical analyses of pacifism and just war approaches beginning from the gospels and continuing with a focus on several major theological thinkers (Tertullian, Origen, Augustine, Aquinas, Luther and Calvin). Detailed consideration is also given to the Crusades, Anabaptist and Quaker traditions and--in the more direct consideration of peacebuilding—Reinhold Niebuhr, Dietrich Bonhoeffer and Dorothy Day. What Cahill is trying to do, I think, is work past the opposition between pacifist and just war approaches. This 'moving beyond' is partly directed by attention to the moral task of peacebuilding itself rather than consideration of two contrasting moral approaches. Indeed, she regards pacifism as less a moral theory than 'a practice—an ongoing communal way of life' founded in 'the reality of a transformed life embodied in Christ and enabled in the church by his Spirit' (17). Attention is focussed thereby on the 'positive and nonviolent cultivation of peace' (1) but without any insistence on the purity of the pacifist response. (In this regard, Cahill might find part of Douglas's argument congenial.) In the peacebuilding approach there is therefore an emphasis on political authority but politics is construed broadly as 'involving "on the ground" efforts by people in communities where the effects of war and violence are most acutely felt' (6). As such, Cahill argues that 'Peacebuilding is the rightful heir of Christian just war and pacifism, in that it is embodied in evangelical communities of peace and reconciliation; transforms societies by upholding the rule of (just) law, democratic participation, and restorative justice; and builds alliances among the many faiths and cultures that together are marred by violence and together must overcome it' (19).

The last two chapters are devoted to the amplification of peacebuilding, seeking orientation for the 'irreducible moral dilemma' that is the 'clash of the duty to save and protect the innocent and the common good, as well as the duty to respect the value and dignity of every human life, including that of the perpetrator and of those who suffer the collateral damage of war' (286). Cahill introduces Niebuhr, Bonhoeffer, Day and recent papal encyclicals as intermediate steps towards a Christian understanding of peacebuilding. Her summary is as follows: 'Christian peacebuilders embrace gospel nonviolence as part of their active commitment to transform conflict and make the reign of God more visible under historically imperfect conditions' (326). Although violence is not always to be rejected, 'They [peacebuilders] focus not on possible justifications of violence, but on promising strategies of building just and peaceful societies in difficult circumstances' (326). Nonetheless, the focus here is on human persons in their communities and societies. Although at one point, Cahill notes that violence leaves deep wounds yet there is no acknowledgment of ecological violence or of the ways in which ecological matters must inform a durable peace.

At the core of both these books is a concern with peace. Douglas works within the contrast of pacifism and just war whereas Cahill suggests peacebuilding as a possible alternative to this contrast. Douglas also calls into question the standard narrative and periodisation associated with the importance of pacifism to the western churches. Both would certainly agree that there will be no longer-term and sustainable future without 'peace with nature'. Indeed, perhaps we are seeing here evidence of the start of a longer-term—and hopeful—reorientation of Christian political ethics for the age of the Anthropocene.

Peter Manley Scott, Lincoln Theological Institute, University of Manchester

The Oxford Handbook of Reinhold Niebuhr

Ed. Robin Lovin and Joshua Mauldin
Oxford University Press, 2021, xix + 637pp, hbk, £110.00

On first encounter, the title has a curious feel, almost implying that Niebuhr carried this book around with him wherever he went! On reading the book, however, the title does describe precisely what this volume says it is. It is not a dictionary of Niebuhr nor is it simply an encyclopaedic review. Instead, it is a rich collection of essays which would helpfully accompany any scholar working on Niebuhr, at virtually any level, or indeed anyone encountering him for the first time. It is divided into six sections - Niebuhr and his times; Allies and Adversaries; Theological starting points; Ethics; Politics and Policy; and Niebuhr's Legacy. The varied and specialised nature of the contributors is impressive.

Healan Gaston's opening essay on Niebuhr's background is immensely useful and sets the scene well, both concisely and with lucidity. This is followed by four essays on the key periods that Niebuhr's work addressed. Jeremy Sabella starts with the 1930s and Moral Man and Immoral Society. He discusses whether Niebuhr's work is inconsistent or simply developmental over the decades, looking at the limits of liberalism and outlining his brother, Richard Niebuhr's critique of Moral Man and Immoral Society. Graeme Smith takes on the theme of 'Global War' introducing both The Nature and Destiny of Man and The Children of Light and the Children of Darkness. Andrew Finstuen picks up the ironies of American power and so The Ironies of American History, following this with mention of Niebuhr's ecumenical work with the foundation of the World Council of Churches in the late 1940s. Finstuen moves to the 1950s and 1960s; he interestingly notes Niebuhr's admiration for James Madison's writing on 'Christian Realism', which he compares with Thomas Jefferson's romantic vision. It was Madison, he argues, who set the American Constitution's checks and balances; he also adverts to Niebuhr's admiration for Abraham Lincoln's realism. Finally, in this first section, Gary Dorrien points to Niebuhr's severe illness in the 1950s and how despite this he continued to contribute - particularly to political debate influencing a vast circle of friends.

In section two, eight interlocutors are reviewed including H Richard Niebuhr, Karl Barth, George Kennan, John Dewey, Paul Tillich, John Courtney Murray, Abraham Heschel and Martin Luther King Jr. Some adversaries came into sharper combat than others; Richard Niebuhr had much sympathy and admiration for his brother, but was not fearful of pointing to weaknesses. So, for example, with Moral Man and Immoral Society Richard was more critical and argued that ultimately, Reinie remained tainted with the same liberalism of which he was so critical. With Barth, Joshua Mauldin indicates a wide gulf between the two of them, including some waspish encounters; a clear statement of Niebuhr's critique of Barth is included. With Kennan there was much common ground on 'realism' although the two of them hardly met! Daniel Rice points to John Dewey's 'social liberalism' which was combined with a religious scepticism - the two disagreed over their understandings of 'naturalism'. Adam Pryor notes Tillich and Niebuhr's strong support for each other earlier in their careers. Later they diverged, particularly on their understandings of Luther and Kierkegaard; ultimately, a mutual constructive critique emerged particularly relating to creation and fall. Encountering John Courtney Murray, softened some of Niebuhr's anti-Catholic prejudices and his

Book Reviews

general dismissal of natural law mutated into a better understanding of that current of thought. It is fascinating to read Susannah Heschel's account of her father's engagement and friendship with Niebuhr; there were some close agreements on Niebuhr's argument in MMIS. Martin Luther King was, of course, of a later generation, although Peter Paris points to Niebuhr's influence on King.

The third section investigates Niebuhr's theological writing on particular themes, namely God, Sin, Love, Christology, Ecclesiology and Eschatology. Hauerwas' Christological critique appears once again. On ecclesiology, the general critique of Niebuhr's weaknesses here is noted, although David True defends him to some degree. A similar thematic approach is used in the fourth section on ethics, focusing on Moral Realism; Human Nature and Moral Norms; Justice; Responsibility; Tragedy and Irony; Feminism, and Democracy. Moral realism is reborn with Niebuhr, and his engagement with politics is part of this. The fifth section picks out key topics within the political sphere, ranging from violence, pacifism and the use of force to the family, sexuality and society. Niebuhr's historical contextualising is a key theme, as once again is his focus on tragedy.

Interestingly enough, it is the final brief section on his legacy that produces some material of enduring value and reaching well beyond Niebuhr's own portfolio. So, Stanley Hauerwas' partial reassessment of his own critique of Niebuhr is fascinating. His theological critique remains, but he sets out a most interesting outline of Niebuhr's unique insight and of the nature of 'insight' itself. Hauerwas concludes: 'Those of us who live in his wake are in his debt.' Jeffrey Stout contributes an equally important assessment on the 'ironies of proximate justice', concluding that proximate justice is insufficient on its own. Then, John Bew offers a remarkable piece, comparing first of all Burke and Niebuhr and their respective impacts. His analysis of recent American history in the light of this is sobering. Sadly, Robin Lovin's concluding essay is too brief to allow this consummate Niebuhrian commentator sufficient space for an effective critique.

In all, however, this volume is a tour de force and a most admirable handbook to a theologian, moralist and political commentator whose influence just will not die away!

Stephen Platten, Berwick-upon-Tweed

Book Reviews

How do I Look? Theology in the Age of the Selfie
Dominic White
SCM Press, 2021, 256pp, pbk, £25

At the time of reading this book there is ongoing uncertainty about Covid and how far it will continue to impact on daily living as winter approaches. At one level, however, nothing changes, as the machinery of modern life continues to move and sustain us. The mobile phone, our laptops, and the availability of Wi-Fi in these pandemic times have all been an essential part of our toolkit for survival.

In all this what do we think it means to be human? Where is God to be found, if at all, in these fragile times? What might we have learnt about ourselves, what is important and how we relate? There are many who might wonder what these months will bring and what we need to recover to flourish. There are some who point out that the poverty of modernity exposes fault lines, idols and even demons that we need to deal with if life is to have purpose.

At Sarum College we believe that theology has a generative place in enabling us to understand who we are and what kind of world we live in. Dominic White - a scholar, pastor and musician - is a friar of the Order of Preachers. This book is a creative contribution to a theology that invites us into reflecting on how we relate within the context of our call to participate in the divine nature.

Some say that the pace of life has accelerated to such an extent that we are less inclined to be able to stand still and attend to the moment. In this moment we might ask ourselves what it is that captures our attention and how we nurture the gift of presence and being omits such hyperactivity. White argues that in the age of the retouchable selfie the impact of this culture on young people is deep and far-reaching. The obsession with how we present ourselves is a constant challenge to those of us who seek to navigate the world of social media.

In these eight chapters (note some of their titles –'How do I look? Seeing and (not) being seen'; 'The face of God and the gaze of Jesus'; 'Seeing God, seeing our neighbour') the reader is invited into an exploration of the long tradition of the Christian gaze. How can this tradition, found in scripture, art, theology, and philosophy, speak into this selfie generation? Grounded in the doctrine of humankind's creation in God's image and the Incarnation, we are taken beyond the masks we wear into an invitation to participate, to know and to be

Book Reviews

aware of what limits and diminishes us in the selfie culture. In short, we are asked to consider what it means to be transfigured.

This is theology at its best – deep, wide, engaged and nourished by a tradition that is orthodox, creative, and progressive. If you want to find our more, look at the recording of the launch of the book from the Margaret Beaufort Institute.

James Woodward, Sarum College

SCM Studyguide to Anglicanism (2nd Edition)
Stephen Spencer
SCM Press, 2021, xii+275pp, pbk, £19.99

What is Anglicanism? What is it about? These are not easy questions to answer, especially when one considers the extent to which the Anglican Communion in the global context is of much greater interest to theologians and students of theology today than it once was. Although this second edition of the SCM Studyguide to Anglicanism does not engage with any big philosophical theories of post-colonialism and decolonisation, Stephen Spencer (Director of Theological Education at the Anglican Communion Office) has nonetheless represented the broader picture of Anglicanism in this studyguide, and assumes that Anglican faith and community will continue to develop in diverse and varied directions.

In the first part of the book, Spencer focuses on the development of Anglican faith and begins with the doctrine of God's grace—the most prominent theological theme of the Reformation. He explains how Martin Luther's rediscovery of justification by faith led to Protestantism and how, having adopted this theological idea, post-Cranmerian Anglicanism placed greater emphasis on the association of grace with love. Chapter 2 reflects on how Anglican faith is formed by Scripture (in particular, vernacular translations of the Bible), by tradition (expressed in the applied use of the prayer book) and by reason (as shown in Hooker and his notion of natural law). Chapter 3 demonstrates three forms of faith expression—by the reasoning mind, by the heart and by the imagination. These are exemplified by the rationality of Joseph Butler and William Law, the emotion of the Wesleys and the Evangelical revival (together with the modern charismatic movement), and the artistic creativity of Samuel Taylor

Book Reviews

Coleridge and Evelyn Underhill.

In the second part of the book, Spencer focuses his attention on the Anglican community. In Chapter 4, he notes that, in Britain, the community is centred on catholic sacramentality, rooted in the catholic prayer book tradition, the High Church movement and the creation of the Scottish Liturgy. In Chapter 5 he goes into further detail about the Oxford Movement and the formation of a distinctive community based on Apostolic authority and welcoming and serving the excluded. Spencer also examines how Anglican communities became more 'distinctive' as they gradually separated from political authorities. Chapter 6 introduces the reader to the role of the Anglican community in different contexts—the Anglican churches in North America as settler churches; within the Church of South India as a minority (and as an ecumenical and united body); and the Anglican churches in East and West Africa as majorities. Spencer also highlights how Anglican communities in different regions grew along different lines, developing different strengths and forming their own distinct identities.

In the third part of the book, Spencer presents various themes associated with the Anglican mission. Chapter 7 outlines three ways of proclaiming the gospel—preaching and conversion, liturgical performance and worship, and social action and ecumenical dialogues (exemplified by F. D. Maurice). Chapter 8 highlights three ministries of charity in responding to human needs—working for the poor in Victorian Britain, organising and supporting women, and empowering the abused across the world. Chapter 9 further shows how Anglican communities engage with social transformation in the fields of education (Sunday school, national education and adult education) and the reformation of social structures (supported by the movement of Christian Socialism and William Temple). In the last example, Spencer takes time to emphasise the urgent concern with environmental issues and how it has become such an important component of a truly holistic understanding of mission, becoming elevated to one of the Five Marks of Mission of the Anglican Communion and providing a clear demonstration of the crucial missional commitment to 'sustain and renew the life of the earth'.

In the final part of the book, Spencer explains the instruments of communion—the role of the Archbishop of Canterbury, the Lambeth Conference, and the Anglican Consultative Council. These explanations help us understand the nature of fellowship in the Anglican Communion and how such fellowship is formed and maintained.

This is a very informative and accessible textbook for all levels of readers. It helpfully incorporates different contexts and experiences of Anglican churches outside the Church of England. With its strong focus on global Anglicanism beyond the Church of England it is a timely publication ahead of the Lambeth Conference in 2022. It also provides a useful snapshot of the diversity of the Anglican Communion in the 21st century. Refreshingly, the book does not conform to traditional Anglican textbook structure—neither offering a historical chronicle from Celtic Christianity onwards (through the Reformation, to the modern Anglicanism Communion), nor structured around the Anglican three-legged stool of Scripture, tradition, and reason. The book is instead an 'exploration' that starts out with core faith, traversing community and mission and concluding with the organisational structure of the global Anglican communion. Spencer's methodology shows how the 'common' Anglican faith is shared by different voices (liberal and conservative) and by different traditions (high church and low church). Despite the presence of different strategies (both individual and collective), it is not divided by theological tribalism.

In addition, as each chapter unfolds the history of Anglicanism, the reader gradually begins to sense how Anglican faith evolved from its English origin and then spread beyond the British Isles. There is, however, potential for theological concern, as Spencer appears to support the notion that the core of Anglicanism remains, at its core, essentially English, despite its diversification into many different expressions as it has spread worldwide. For example, Spencer rarely mentions any Anglican 'faith' outside the Church of England but heavily emphasises different missions and ministries when Anglicanism is applied in different contexts. Further questioning is worthwhile as to Spencer's underlying assumption that global Anglicanism consists merely of plural expressions of 'English' Anglicanism.

Yin-An Chen, Cambridge Centre for Christianity Worldwide

CHEQUE OR CREDIT CARD		DIRECT DEBIT	
Individual rate UK:	☐ £22	☐ £20	
Institutional rate UK:	☐ £40	☐ £35	
Individual international:	☐ £40		
Institutional international:	☐ £50		
Individual copy	☐ £7		

Crucible

Please complete section 1. Cheque **or** 2. Credit/Debit card **or** 3. Direct debit
(the name and address you give must match the information on your credit/Debit card/bank statement.)

YOUR DETAILS (Please complete]

Title ....Christian name ....Surname ....

Address: ....

....

....

Postcode .... Daytime telephone no ....

Email: ....

- I enclose a cheque for the total amount of £.............. payable to Hymns Ancient and Modern Ltd.
- To pay by credit/debit card please visit www.cruciblejournal.co.uk/subscribe or contact us on 01603 785911

HYMNS Ancient & Modern

Instruction to your bank or building society to pay by Direct Debit

DIRECT Debit

Please fill in the whole form using a ball point pen and send to:
Hymns Ancient & Modern Ltd.

Name and full postal address of your bank or building society

To: The Manager   Bank/building society

Address

Postcode

Name(s) of account holder(s)

Bank/building society account number

Branch sort code

Service user number: 2 4 3 2 3 3

Reference

Instruction to your bank or building society
Please pay Hymns Ancient & Modern Ltd Direct Debits from the account detailed in this Instruction subject to the safeguards assured by the Direct Debit Guarantee. I understand that this instruction may remain with Hymns Ancient & Modern Ltd and, if so, details will be passed electronically to my bank/building society.

Hymns Ancient & Modern Ltd, 13a Hellesdon Park Road, Norwich NR6 5DR

Signature(s)

Banks and building societies may not accept Direct Debit Instructions for some types of account.

This Guarantee should be detached and retained by the payer.

The Direct Debit Guarantee

DIRECT Debit

- This Guarantee is offered by all banks and building societies that accept instructions to pay Direct Debits
- If there are any changes to the amount, date or frequency of your Direct Debit Hymns Ancient & Modern Ltd will notify you 10 working days in advance of your account being debited or as otherwise agreed. If you request Hymns Ancient & Modern Ltd to collect payment, confirmation of the amount and date will be given to you at the time of the request
- If an error is made in the payment of your Direct Debit, by Hymns Ancient & Modern Ltd or your bank or building society, you are entitled to a full and immediate refund of the amount paid from your bank or building society
  - If you receive a refund you are not entitled to, you must pay it back when Hymns Ancient & Modern Ltd asks you to
- You can cancel a Direct Debit at any time by simply contacting your bank or building society. Written confirmation may be required. Please also notify us

www.ingramcontent.com/pod-product-compliance
Lightning Source LLC
Chambersburg PA
CBHW022022290426
44109CB00015B/1270